Studying P

Studying Poetry

An Introduction

R. T. JONES
Senior Lecturer in English,
University of York

Edward Arnold

A division of Hodder & Stoughton

LONDON   NEW YORK   MELBOURNE   AUCKLAND

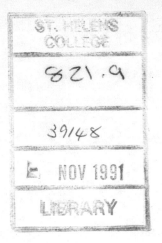

© 1986 R. T. Jones

First published in Great Britain 1986
Reprinted 1987, 1988, 1990

Distributed in the USA by Routledge, Chapman and Hall, Inc.
29 West 35th Street, New York, NY 10001

British Library Cataloguing in Publication Data

Jones, R. T.
  Studying poetry: an introduction.
  1. English poetry—Study and teaching
  I. Title
  821′.007   PR504.5

  ISBN 0–7131–6467–0

Typeset in 10/11pt Cheltenham Book Compugraphic by Colset Pte
Ltd, Singapore. Printed and bound in Great Britain for Edward
Arnold, a division of Hodder and Stoughton Limited, Mill Road,
Dunton Green, Sevenoaks, Kent TN13 2YA by Clays Ltd, St Ives
plc.

Contents

Acknowledgements   vi
1   Introductory Definitions   1
2   The Value of Poetry   5
3   Imagery and Rhythm   22
4   Meaning   42
5   In Different Voices   58
Index   73

Acknowledgements

The publishers would like to thank the following for their permission to include the following poems: Faber & Faber Publishers Ltd and Alfred A. Knopf Inc. for 'A Dish of Peaches in Russia' from *The Collected Poems of Wallace Stevens*, copyright 1942 by Wallace Stevens and A.P. Watt Ltd for 'Easter 1916' from *Collected Poems of W.B. Yeats* used by permission of Michael B. Yeats and Macmillan, London.

1 Introductory Definitions

> And this
> Is the upper sling swivel, whose use you will see
> When you are given your slings. And this is the piling
>   swivel,
> Which in your case you have not got.
>
> Henry Reed, *Naming of Parts*

A large number of terms that used to be used in the analysis of poetry have fallen into disuse during the present century, and there is no need to regret their loss. Many of them were always misfits when applied to English verse, because they had been developed to describe features of classical Latin verse, which was different in quite important ways. An elaborate system of specialized terms is not necessary anyway for understanding or discussing poetry (nearly all of which was written for non-specialists); one thing that I hope to show in this book is that we can go a long way without bothering about spondees and dactyls. Still, there are a few terms that are likely to be used quite often, so it is necessary that we should mean the same things by them.

Rarely, poetry may be in *prose* – as, for example, in the opening pages of D. H. Lawrence's novel *The Rainbow*. Prose is simply any writing in which the author does not make expressive use of line-endings, but leaves it to every copyist – typist or compositor – to divide each paragraph into lines such as will make the page look tidy (usually with a straight margin on each side).

When a writer wants to exert more control over the way his words are to be read and spoken, he will often set them out in lines which represent rhythmic groups of spoken words. Any piece of writing so set out – where the writer has settled where the line-divisions are to be – is called *verse*. (Whether or not it is poetry is another question, involving a value judgement; but the use of verse usually signals a wish on the part of the author that the words should be read as poetry.)

If a passage of verse, when read aloud, reveals no constant rhythmic pattern, no regular arrangement of stressed and unstressed syllables, though strongly marked rhythms may occur within it, it is called *free verse*. An example is the excerpt from D. H. Lawrence's *Kangaroo* on page 36. Since the publication of T. S. Eliot's *The Waste Land* in 1922, free verse has been widely practised; it was rarely used in earlier centuries.

A regular arrangement of stressed and unstressed syllables is a *metre*, or measure. The most usual in English is the line of ten syllables, stressed on alternate syllables starting with the second, as in the line

And put his life between the judge's lips

in the passage by Tourneur quoted on page 23. It is no longer necessary for the student of English poetry to know Greek names for English metres, but this one is so common that it is useful to have a name for it, so it goes on being called the *iambic pentameter*. Most of Chaucer's *Canterbury Tales*, all but the last line of each stanza of Spenser's *Faerie Queene*, nearly all the verse in Shakespeare's plays, Milton's *Paradise Lost*, Pope's satires and Wordsworth's *Prelude*, among others, are in iambic pentameters.

This does not mean that every line in these works is strictly an iambic pentameter. There can be many variations; one or two syllables may be omitted or added, one or two of the stresses may occur earlier or later than expected, but the reader may still be kept aware of the iambic pentameter as the underlying pattern of the work. Because this metre is so familiar to every reader of English poetry, we recognize it even when most of the lines diverge from the basic pattern – and, as we shall see when we look closely at particular examples, it is the divergences that then become significant.

When, as in most of Shakespeare's dramatic verse, the iambic pentameters do not rhyme, they are called *blank verse*. (This should not be confused with *free verse*, which is non-metrical as well as unrhymed.) The passage from *The Revenger's Tragedy* by Tourneur on page 23 is in blank verse.

If the iambic pentameters rhyme in pairs, as they do in

Chaucer's tales and in Pope's satires, the verse is said to be in *heroic couplets* ('heroic' only because this metre was in the seventeenth century regarded as particularly appropriate for heroic subjects). Milton's *On the University Carrier*, on page 59, is in heroic couplets.

Some pieces of verse are divided into *stanzas* – that is, groups of lines shaped in such a way that every group could be sung to the same tune. Usually this means that every stanza in the same piece has the same number of lines, each line has the same number of stressed syllables as the corresponding line in every other stanza, and if there is rhyme (as there usually is in stanzaic verse), the pattern of rhymes is the same in every stanza. When there are variations they are generally of such a kind that the variant stanza could still be sung to the same tune as the others by repeating a line or two of the tune. Some verse, of course, was composed for singing, like *I sing of a maiden* on page 33; but a great deal of verse that was never intended to be sung has been composed in the form of stanzas and gains some song-like quality by being in that form, like Blake's *A Poison Tree* on page 71.

When a stretch of blank verse, heroic couplets, or other verse is divided into quite irregular sections by indenting the first line of each new section, like paragraphs in prose, these sections are not stanzas; in fact they can simply be called *paragraphs*, as in *Easter 1916* by Yeats on page 17.

A *sonnet* is usually a complete work in itself, and so cannot properly be called a stanza – though this could be arguable when the sonnet is one of a sequence and so, though able to stand alone, forms part of a larger whole. A sonnet has fourteen lines; in the kind that is called Petrarchan, which follows Italian models; there is first a set of eight lines called the *octave* or *octet* in which lines one, four, five and eight rhyme with each other and lines two, three, six and seven rhyme with each other, and then a set of six lines called the *sestet* with a rhyme scheme that, though it need not always be the same, always links the six lines in a single pattern. The Shakespearean sonnet, on the other hand, divides its fourteen lines into three *quatrains* (groups of four lines) and a couplet; there may be a recognizable break between octave and sestet, but the pattern of rhymes does not make one. A Shakespearean sonnet is quoted on page 8.

Many poets have written sonnets, evidently finding the form suitable for some of their most serious work. The shape of the sonnet seems to be adaptable to the presentation of a wide variety of observations. Quite often, for example, the octave presents a state of affairs and the sestet comments on it or interprets it. Probably there is also an element of challenge in the appeal of this form: the poet undertakes to re-think an experience until it can be brought to inhabit the sonnet form with such apparent ease that one could almost believe that the form had been invented to accommodate that particular thought. What is not so obvious is why other equally elaborate verse forms, like the *ballade*, the *rondeau*, and the *sestina*, very rarely in English seem anything but clever exercises. Any reader who is interested may find examples in the early work of Ezra Pound; and it would only be confusing to have definitions without examples.

I have suggested that it is not very useful these days to know names for different metres, with the possible exception of the iambic pentameter. It is unlikely to be helpful, in any discussion today, to say that the metre of *The Song of Hiawatha*, by Longfellow, is trochaic tetrameters, because this will tell most people less than quoting a line or two, and cannot tell anybody more – and the description is very nearly as long as the line it describes:

Then the little Hiawatha. . . .

Given a rather longer extract to consider, we ought to be able to find more informative things to say about the movement of the verse and how, even when it is varied a good deal, it tends to trot along rather monotonously and not to encourage any thoughtful attention to its words.

Some other terms will be used in the chapters that follow, and where they seem to require explanation this will be given as they occur. For the rest, readers are advised to make use of a dictionary.

2 The Value of Poetry

'. . . But do you wish me to attend to what you are going to say?'
'Yes,' replied Belinda, smiling; 'that is the usual wish of those who speak.'

Maria Edgeworth, *Belinda*

One term not defined in Chapter 1 is *poetry*. It seems best not to try to define it. To offer a definition of poetry, which would have to be based on the kinds of poetry I happen to have seen already, would be to limit it to those kinds, and could make it harder to recognize new and unfamiliar kinds of poetry.

Poetry cannot be identified by its shape on the page or by any other external characteristics. To call something a poem is to attribute a value and an importance to it; as Robert Frost said, ' "Poet" is a praise-word.' There is no reason why anybody should not say 'I write verse', but 'I write poetry' is a proud claim and should not be made lightly. It is the critic's task rather than the writer's to say whether what has been written is a poem or not; a writer is not always a good critic of his own work.

We, of course, are the critics. Every reader is a critic, even if the only expression of his judgement is his willingness or reluctance to be interrupted while reading, or the gesture with which he closes the book on reaching the end. We cannot read without judgement; the only choice we have in the matter is whether to be careful and responsible critics or not.

Though I offer no definition of poetry, I hope to show how it can be recognized. We do, after all, recognize many things without having definitions to apply to them – dogs, for instance. I propose to display several different kinds of poem, and suggest why I think they *are* poems. This, as I have said, involves value judgements, with some of which the reader may disagree. That is as it should be, for people do often disagree about whether something is a poem or not. For this reason, a book like this cannot be authoritative; it cannot tell readers *how to* respond to and think about poetry. This book records how one reader responds to and thinks about some poems, in the hope that this may help other readers to find their own ways of doing so – which will be different.

Whatever else a poem is, it is a sequence of words; and as with any other sequence of words that we hear or see, the first thing we have to try to do is to understand them. They may, of course, turn out to be unintelligible, but I think we owe it to the author (as to anybody else who addresses words to us) to start by assuming that he is honestly trying to tell us something. We may in the end find this hypothesis untenable, and have to fall back on the possibility that he is dishonestly trying to tell us something, or that he is trying to obscure something from us, or that what he is offering us is a pattern of shapes on the page or of sounds made in saying the words. But it seems natural to treat the author with the same courtesy as we expect of a friend to whom we speak: to begin by supposing that he is trying to tell something as it really is; that is, to tell the truth.

I shall not, of course, try to say what I mean by 'truth' and 'reality'. Whether we say that there are many different kinds of truth, or that truth has many dimensions, we had better not start with a definition that could make it harder than it need be to recognize modes of truth that we have not previously considered. A poem that begins 'I heard a fly buzz when I died' (as one of Emily Dickinson's does) is perhaps more obviously fictional than most, and it would not be appropriate to suppose that it records a historical fact, but it may still be the best way of communicating a strenuously-achieved insight.

We may value the pursuit of truth in a poem without being convinced by its conclusion. Poets have argued many things – the legitimacy of the Tudor dynasty, the universal fickleness of women, the matchless perfection of one woman, the ability of plants to experience and express pleasure; we may believe that they were mistaken, or we may not think it matters much whether they were or not. But we may value the resourcefulness and intelligence at work in the process of the poet's engagement with problems that are not necessarily our problems.

I hope to show how poetry may make us see things, aspects of reality, that we could not have seen without it, and even, if we read with a sufficiently open mind, make us see truths that we should prefer not to see. But whether the material with which the poet wrestles is relevant to our own concerns or not, we may value the opportunity the poem gives us to follow, and experience, the process by which the poet works towards the clarification of the truth he seeks.

Let us begin, then, by supposing – or at least hoping – that what poetry can do for us is to enable us to participate in the poet's activity of trying hard to capture in words the exact truth as he experiences it. In order to do this it must have the fullest attention we can give. We study a poem not, in the first place, in order to gain knowledge about it, but to gain knowledge from it.

It is not enough to recognize that a poem is beautiful, for that can happen at different levels: it is perfectly possible to say, 'He spoke beautifully, but I didn't understand a word of it'; and I have seen separate pages of a Hebrew Bible bought for the beauty of their appearance, regardless of whether they were fragments of the Book of Job or the genealogies of the Kings of Edom. This is not to deny the importance of beauty in poetry. From the poet's attempt to tell the exact truth, and from the rare perfection of success in the attempt, beauty may emerge, as from many other well-made things and well-achieved activities; it may even be one of the signs by which we can recognize such success. But if we dwell on superficial or incidental beauty in a poem instead of attending carefully to what it is saying, we are likely to miss the richer and more rewarding beauty that comes of a full response to the whole poem.

Anybody who sets out to tell something as it really is (as one can readily verify by trying to write down what one really feels about one's parents) encounters at a very early stage the difficulty of resisting cliché and conventional ideas. The first ideas and phrases that come to mind are likely to be from the available common stock, and to have more to do with what one is expected to feel, what one would like to feel, or what one would wish others to believe one feels, than with what one really does feel. It is never easy to set these aside, both because all communication depends on shared conventions ('I gotta use words when I talk to you'), and because one normally regards one's own behaviour and attitudes as 'natural' and those of other people as 'conventional' – it is hard to recognize as conventions those conventions that one lives by. Sometimes, as in Shakespeare's *Sonnet 130*, the effort to find and tell the truth may require a direct attack on conventions.

My mistress' eyes are nothing like the sun;
Coral is far more red than her lips' red;
If snow be white, why then her breasts are dun;
If hairs be wires, black wires grow on her head.
I have seen roses damasked, red and white,
But no such roses see I in her cheeks,
And in some perfumes is there more delight
Than in the breath that from my mistress reeks.
I love to hear her speak, yet well I know
That music hath a far more pleasing sound.
I grant I never saw a goddess go;
My mistress when she walks treads on the ground.
   And yet, by heaven, I think my love as rare
   As any she belied with false compare.

(The modern reader may need to make a momentary effort to purge the word 'wires' of its associations with electrical and telephonic cables, and to connect it instead with gold wire or thread-of-gold, a conventional comparison for hair. 'She', in the last line, is used contemptuously, as if it were a noun – 'as any female. . . .')

This poem, consisting almost entirely of negations, explicit or implicit, sketches out by suggestion its anti-poem, which would be a compendium of clichés:

My mistress' eyes are like the sun;
Her lips are red as coral;
Her breasts are white as snow;
Her hair is thread-of-gold.
In her cheeks are roses, red and white;
Her breath is the most delightful of perfumes.
Her voice is sweeter than any music,
And she walks like a goddess.

The first quatrain of Shakespeare's sonnet consists of direct denials of the conventional praises. The second starts with 'I have seen roses. . . .', which seems to say, with an air of comic puzzlement, 'I know it's customary to say that one's mistress' cheeks are like roses; but I've taken the rather unusual step of looking at roses and at her cheeks, and I'm bound in honesty to report that I couldn't see any resemblance at all.' Then the caution of '*some* perfumes' leads up to the blunt shock of 'reeks'. Impatience is suggested in the way the speaker spells out the truth, as if determined to make it clear to the foggiest intellect, in 'I love to hear her speak, yet well I know/ That music hath a far more pleasing sound.' When he comes to the conventional comparison of one's mistress to a goddess, in respect of the way she walks, he freely concedes that he hasn't been able to verify this, like the roses, by his own observation, but at least he can assure us that his mistress does not step on clouds.

I referred in the last paragraph to 'the speaker' in the poem, rather than to 'Shakespeare' who wrote the poem, but who may, as far as we know, have been imagining what somebody in a given situation might say. The fact that a poem is written in the first person does not entitle us to assume that it reports auto-biographical events. As long as we bear in mind the possibility that the sonnet is fictional – a dramatic fragment – we shall not be in danger of using it as a springboard for conjectures (or fantasies) about Shakespeare's life and relationships.

We may then, as a way of focusing from a different angle on the nature and effect of the poem, imagine what the lady herself might have thought of it. She might well have been indignant at first, until she realized that every statement in the poem, every refusal to reiterate blindly the conventional terms of praise, and to pay her compliments in the usual currency, pays her in fact the much greater tribute of recognizing her human reality, as a conventional love-poem could not. The speaker has paid her the compliment of looking at her and seeing her as a real person, rather than a stock idea to be poetically decorated with second-hand praises. And false praise is not kind: it makes the recipient uncomfortably – even guiltily – aware of failing to measure up to it. Infinitely preferable, surely, is the warm appreciation of the lady for being what she is, expressed in the line

My mistress when she walks treads on the ground.

Of course there is much more to be said about this poem. We ought to notice how the ferocity of the closing couplet, the challenge to all comers, is given weight by the clear-eyed appreciation that has preceded it. And we could consider how much deeper the defiance of convention goes than the simple rejection of verbal clichés – the way in which the poem, by affirming a love that is not dependent on the listed externals, mocks the kind of love that does depend on such things as the lady's pigmentation and the lover's capacity for inexact observation. But I have said enough for my present purpose, which is to present this poem as a fairly clear example of the poet's primary concern with truth, with the attempt to see things as they really are. One could perhaps talk about this poem in terms of its beauty, and this might be useful at a late stage in the discussion: one would have to distinguish between the beauty the poem rejects, the beauty it affirms, and the beauty (if that is the right word) of the affirmation. But it seems to me that the value of the poem is that it brings us to experience for a moment what it feels like to have the courage to see the truth, and the audacity to tell it, however disconcerting it might be; and to perform this grim but unexpectedly rewarding task with a certain teasing gaiety.

My next example, Shakespeare's *Sonnet 138*, is more painful, and brings no comforting affirmation in its tail. It is a greater poem in that the truth it investigates is more complex and harder to tell.

When my love swears that she is made of truth,
I do believe her though I know she lies,
That she might think me some untutored youth,
Unlearnèd in the world's false subtleties.
Thus vainly thinking that she thinks me young,
Although she knows my days are past the best,
Simply I credit her false-speaking tongue;
On both sides thus is simple truth suppressed.
But wherefore says she not she is unjust?
And wherefore say not I that I am old?
O, love's best habit is in seeming trust,
And age in love loves not to have years told.
   Therefore I lie with her, and she with me,
   And in our faults by lies we flattered be.

It is generally worth starting a discussion of a poem with an outline of what one supposes it to be about. It is not often safe to assume agreement about this. Disagreements about the value of a work of literature often turn out to be grounded on different readings, by the opponents, of the words on the page: they have been, in effect, talking about different poems. The difference can often be resolved, in discussion, by carefully attending to the words on the page; and, although there are some who seem to believe that any way in which a poem *can* be read is as valid as any other, it is very often possible to reach agreement that one of the proposed readings is right – or at least that the other is mistaken.

This poem, then, is about a pair of lovers, one of whom, the woman, is false, and the other, the speaker in the poem, is old. He pretends to believe that she is true to him, and even habitually persuades himself that he believes her; and he does this in order to seem simple and inexperienced, so that he can seem young. Neither is taken in by this, though he likes to think that she is. The sequence of mutual deceits seems to stretch on to infinity, like images in a pair of confronting mirrors. She knows that he knows that she knows . . . while each pretends not to know at all. A chain of falsehood has been constructed, in which the falsehood of each is condoned by the other, because it has become necessary to each. But why, he asks, do they not end this horrible sequence by freely admitting, she that she deceives him, and he that he is old? The answer is that in order that love may continue, it is necessary for them to preserve an appearance of trust and an illusion of youth. No doubt trust and youth would be better, but in the relationship here presented these are not available; one has to start from where one is; the only choice here is between the counterfeit of these qualities and their manifest absence. The illusion and the appearance are better than nothing.

So the relationship rests upon lies that deceive neither of the lovers, except in so far as they choose to deceive themselves. And the pun in the closing couplet is no mere ornament. It shows falsehood as being present, inextricably, at the very centre of their love: even at the moment of physical union – a moment when, if ever, pretences might be laid aside – even then this relationship is a sharing of lies: the lying and the lying-with are one.

The lucid precision of the analysis suggests the outcome of a strenuous activity of bringing concealed and self-deceiving

motives out of muddy obscurity into sharp clarity. When it is all
clear, it brings no solution: the pain is increased by the fact that
it is clearly going to continue. Yet pain is not what the poem
leaves with us; if it were simply that, we could hardly wish to
read it again, or to go on to read others. What we have in this
sonnet is pain transmuted into a made thing, an artefact; so that
the form of the sonnet, with its systematic progression from
quatrain to quatrain, clinched by the couplet, is itself an affirmation of the poet's control over the experience. As Donne
says in *The Triple Fool*,

Grief brought to numbers cannot be so fierce,
For he tames it, that fetters it in verse.

The overwhelming is mastered by being brought into a shape, a
pattern; and an important part of the reader's response is
delight at the neat ordering of the statements – each phrase or
clause forming a ten-syllable line with no strain, as if it spontaneously happened that way, and pairs of lines answering
pairs of lines that rhyme with them. And the final couplet,
though (as I insisted above) no mere ornament. nevertheless *is*
ornament: its wit is the knot that ties up the poem.

There is nothing wonderful about writing a sonnet: all we
have to do is put together some words that make lines of the
right length and approximately the same rhythmic pattern, and
rhyme with each other according to the prescribed formula.
But it is very unlikely that the result would be a poem. Most of us
would fulfil the requirements of a sonnet by bending what we
had to say, contenting ourselves with something less than the
truth; whatever we set out to say would be distorted by the
demands of rhyme and metre. What is impressive in a sonnet
that is also a poem, as these of Shakespeare's are, is that the
sonnet form seems not to be a set of rules imposed on, and dis-
torting, what is to be said, but strikes us rather as a way of
saying it more exactly, more fully, and more clearly.

As I suggested earlier, there is no need to suppose that
Shakespeare, in his sonnets, was writing directly about events
in his own life. He did, we may remind ourselves, write plays;
obviously not every 'I' in his poetry is William Shakespeare. But
this poem can still be recognizably valid as pursuit of truth
without being autobiographical. To have experienced something imaginatively is no less to have experienced it, if the

imagining is done fully and honestly. In fact I doubt whether one does *experience* the things that happen to one, until one *imagines* them. Suppose that this poem were the outcome of the writer's thinking about the condition of two people he knew; *they* might be perfectly complacent about it, quite unaware of the extent of the tangle of deceit and self-deception in which their relationship exists. To them it only happens; it is the poet who experiences it, sees it, and suffers it. Experiencing is an active process.

If we had some means of knowing that Shakespeare's *Sonnet 138* was autobiographical, what would it tell us about him – that he was extremely deceitful, or that he was extremely honest?

Both, perhaps. For we are not here dealing with the systematic formulations of logical or mathematical truth, with terms defined in such a way that two propositions that contradict each other cannot both be true. Dramatic poetry is particularly well adapted to display the complexity of human experience: it can command our assent to the proposition that life is like *this*, and shortly afterwards command our equal assent to the proposition that life is not at all like this, but like *that*. A very simple example of a dramatic poem is Blake's *The Clod and the Pebble*:

'Love seeketh not Itself to please,
Nor for itself hath any care;
But for another gives its ease,
And builds a Heaven in Hell's despair.'

  So sang a little Clod of Clay,
  Trodden with the cattles feet;
  But a Pebble of the brook
  Warbled out these metres meet.

'Love seeketh only Self to please,
To bind another to Its delight:
Joys in anothers loss of ease,
And builds a Hell in Heavens despite.'

Here Blake brings together two contradictory aspects of love – the one that the sentimentalist sees and the one that the cynic sees. We have all heard both views expressed before, in various forms, but here we are made to look at them side by side. What first makes this an uncomfortable experience is that the two have the same form, suggesting that they are the two sides of the same thing, and that if we reject one of them we may find that we are at the same time rejecting the other. If we say, as many readers even today will wish to say, 'The first is what I mean by love – there must be a different name for the second', we are likely to find that we have adopted a one-eyed view of the subject. The almost unimaginable lover who fits the first account will need a partner who fits the second; for there can be no satisfaction or point in sacrificing one's ease for another person, unless that other person derives some joy from the sacrifice. Even if we do not limit the scope of the generalization to human love, but try to see the first account as applying to divine love, we find the same inadequacy; for the loving God must be supposed to take pleasure in the martyrdom, or lesser sacrifices, of the faithful; and they in their turn joy in the crucifixion – a loss of ease if ever there was one. So particular loves, or love in general, can not be adequately seen in either of these ways, but can often seem to be describable in both ways; we might say, 'It all depends which way you look at it.' Blake obliges us to consider both views together, to see love from two points of view simultaneously, so that a more whole and a more complex truth may emerge from the tension between two contradictory statements.

Our minds have some experience in dealing with such tensions. Most of us have two eyes, which continually present us with a pair of more or less contradictory accounts of objects, because they register images of those objects from more or less different angles. The muscular effort of swivelling the eyeballs to co-ordinate the two images, so as to achieve a compatibility between them, is what gives us our sense of comparative distances and of the depth of things. This happens all the time, usually without our needing to think about it; but the same principle is applied when we estimate or calculate the distance or height of an object by taking bearings on it from two different places.

Of course this poem is an extreme case, for the two views that it presents are diametrically opposed, and this makes it exceptionally difficult, perhaps impossible, to achieve effective binocular vision – to see both as one thing. The two speakers in the poem are presented with precise and symmetrical impartiality.

(The word 'meet', meaning 'fitting', might seem to favour the pebble's view, but I do not think it really represents a lapse from impartiality: *those* lines are 'meet', appropriate, to the pebble, which is cold and hard and unimpressible, whereas the first stanza is equally meet to the clod of clay, which owes its form and identity entirely to the successive pressures of the cattle's feet). So we are left to attempt a feat of optical acrobatics: to see the two opposite faces of a thing simultaneously and see it as a single thing. While we strive unsuccessfully for the total vision, we may be impelled to ponder whether, if we have to settle for something less than wholeness, we would prefer to be a pebble, or a clod of clay.

A more representative, and less systematic, example of the juxtaposition of different points of view can be found in Shakespeare's *Henry IV Part 1*, where we are given two opposing views of honour. In Act 1 scene 3, Hotspur says:

By heaven methinks it were an easy leap
To pluck bright honour from the pale-fac'd moon,
Or dive into the bottom of the deep,
Where fathom-line could never touch the ground,
And pluck up drowned honour by the locks;
So he that doth redeem her thence might wear
Without corrival all her dignities. . . .

Later, in Act 5 scene 1, before the battle of Shrewsbury, Falstaff is teasingly reminded by the prince that he owes God a death. Left alone, Falstaff reflects on his lack of eagerness to pay this debt:

'Tis not due yet: I would be loath to pay him before his day. What need I be so forward with him that calls not on me? Well, 'tis no matter; honour pricks me on. Yea, but how if honour prick me off when I come on? how then? Can honour set to a leg? No. Or an arm? No. Or take away the grief of a wound? No. Honour hath no skill in surgery, then? No. What is honour? A word. What is in that word, honour? Air. A trim reckoning! Who hath it? He that died o' Wednesday. Doth he feel it? No. Doth he hear it? No. It is insensible, then? Yea, to the dead. But will it not live with the living? No. Why? Detraction will not suffer it. Therefore I'll none of it: honour is a mere scutcheon; and so ends my catechism.

In their contexts, if they are appropriately read or acted, these two speeches equally command assent. At the end of each we are likely to feel, Yes: it is so. And even reflection cannot wholly convince us that Hotspur is not magnificently right – nor that Falstaff is not refreshingly clear-eyed. Of course we can readily find arguments against each, and we should probably not wish either view to be universally held. But the fact remains that in reading or listening to Hotspur's lines we are participating in an experience of high chivalry, the splendour of which it would be hard not to feel; and that Falstaff's argument is both liberating and unanswerable in its own terms. The important consequence is that after entering into both experiences, we are unlikely to be quite satisfied with either view in its simple, unmixed form; we are impelled to try to reach a view of honour that acknowledges both aspects – a three-dimensional view of what honour is: one eye seeing, as it were, a different image from the other. This is in part what the play is about – the education of the future King Henry V through his dealings with Hotspur and with Falstaff – both of whom he values, and neither of whom he finally accepts (he kills Hotspur and rejects Falstaff). So he, as Henry V, has a far more complex sense of what honour is: he values it as highly as Hotspur does, but is no more dazzled by it than Falstaff is. His mastery is a result of his having known, assimilated and moved beyond both the maniacal egoistic idealism of Hotspur and the grotesque cowardly realism of Falstaff.

The circumstances in which we have to do most of our thinking do not display alternative views to us as clearly as this. Thinking and judging in the thick of events – events in which we may ourselves be involved – our conscious thinking is generally guided by our wishes, our often unacknowleged motives, so that we find ourselves arriving at the conclusion we wished to arrive at, the conclusion that accords with the position we have already committed ourselves to, the conclusion that serves our own interests or our own self-esteem. In the process, we are likely to suppress those truths that oppose the conclusion we want to arrive at, perhaps without knowing that we are doing so.

Here is a poem that seems to me to resist that impulse, and also to explore some of the implications of an obsessive commitment to a cause: *Easter 1916* , by W. B. Yeats. Some preliminary explanations may be necessary, for the poem assumes that its title will mean something to its readers. Briefly, then: the British government had already, in 1914, decided to give home rule to Ireland, but had deferred its implementation until the war against Germany should be over. But there were strong reasons for doubting whether the government would, or could, when the time came, use the necessary military force to put this policy into effect, against very substantial armed resistance in the northern counties of Ireland. The Easter Rising of 1916 in Dublin was organized by the movement for Irish independence. The rebellion was crushed, and sixteen of its leaders were shot. The Countess Markievicz was among those sentenced to death, but her sentence was commuted to life imprisonment; she was released in 1917. Yeats had not taken the revolutionaries seriously before the event; he and his friends had regarded them as unrealistic fanatics. After the executions the Sinn Fein movement spread rapidly.

Easter 1916

I have met them at close of day
Coming with vivid faces
From counter or desk among grey
Eighteenth-century houses.
I have passed with a nod of the head
Or polite meaningless words,
Or have lingered awhile and said
Polite meaningless words,
And thought before I had done
Of a mocking tale or a gibe
To please a companion
Around the fire at the club,
Being certain that they and I
But lived where motley is worn:
All changed, changed utterly:
A terrible beauty is born.

That woman's days were spent
In ignorant good-will,
Her nights in argument
Until her voice grew shrill.

What voice more sweet than hers
When, young and beautiful,
She rode to harriers?
This man had kept a school
And rode our wingèd horse;
This other his helper and friend
Was coming into his force;
He might have won fame in the end,
So sensitive his nature seemed,
So daring and sweet his thought.
This other man I had dreamed
A drunken, vainglorious lout.
He had done most bitter wrong
To some who are near my heart,
Yet I number him in the song;
He, too, has resigned his part
In the casual comedy;
He, too, has been changed in his turn,
Transformed utterly:
A terrible beauty is born.

Hearts with one purpose alone
Through summer and winter seem
Enchanted to a stone
To trouble the living stream.
The horse that comes from the road,
The rider, the birds that range
From cloud to tumbling cloud,
Minute by minute they change;
A shadow of cloud on the stream
Changes minute by minute;
A horse-hoof slides on the brim,
And a horse plashes within it;
The long-legged moor-hens dive,
And hens to moor-cocks call;
Minute by minute they live:
The stone's in the midst of all.

Too long a sacrifice
Can make a stone of the heart.
O when may it suffice?
That is Heaven's part, our part
To murmur name upon name,

As a mother names her child
When sleep at last has come
On limbs that had run wild.
What is it but nightfall?
No, no, not night but death;
Was it needless death after all?
For England may keep faith
For all that is done and said.
We know their dream; enough
To know they dreamed and are dead;
And what if excess of love
Bewildered them till they died?
I write it out in a verse –
MacDonagh and MacBride
And Connolly and Pearse
Now and in time to be,
Wherever green is worn,
Are changed, changed utterly:
A terrible beauty is born.

In the first place, the poem records the change in the speaker's judgement, not only of the rebels, but of the world that he and they inhabited. Their deaths have compelled him to abandon his sense of that world as a trivial one in which only comic roles were available, and to make a sudden and radical adjustment of his sense of what being human can mean.

There is a mocking habit of mind that refuses to acknowledge the seriousness of anything, refuses to see anything as really mattering. It is a limited kind of scepticism. The poem goes beyond that to a more thorough scepticism that can doubt its own validity and admit the possibility of the heroic. The description of the speaker's conviction before the Easter Rising –

Being certain that they and I
But lived where motley is worn

– is a description of a complacently limited view, a one-eyed view of the possibilities of life. The outcome of the event is not a denial of the comic, but a shattering of that certainty that the rebels and he could *only* inhabit a comic world.

The second part of the poem suggests how each of the people concerned appears to the speaker in retrospect; and although there is no mockery now, there is also no attempt to portray them as potential heroes. Con Markievicz had not died, but she had already given up much of her life – given up, it would seem, the sweetness of life; and there is no idealization of her in the judgement 'in ignorant good-will.' The tribute to the young man who 'might have won fame in the end' points both to regret at the premature closing of that possibility, and to recognition that his rebellion and execution have transformed him into a far more disturbing force than literary 'fame' implies. That the other man 'had done most bitter wrong/ To some who are near my heart' remains a fact that has to be assimilated somehow into the new sense of him – 'Transformed utterly'. The poem suppresses nothing; it leads us through the experience of thinking inclusively.

The third section moves to a certain distance from the events themselves, to question the relation between the committed, or the obsessed, and the variety of life that goes on around them. The judgement that emerges is a complex one, registering both a vivid delight in the ever-changing world of nature and a wonder at the strange and disturbing power of the motionless stone – the dedication to a single purpose that is both an obstruction to the 'living stream' and a fixed point of reference without which the changing world might be a mere succession of random events.

The fourth part comes back to the men who died, and exhibits a questioning, exploratory activity of thought. The analogy with the sleeping child momentarily betrays the speaker into the false consolation that death is only a sleep – 'What is it but nightfall?' – and he recalls himself to the less bearable reality: 'No, no, not night but death;' they are *not* the same. He is not even sure that the Rising was politically necessary. But this is not the point; 'enough/ To know they dreamed and are dead'. The ambiguity of 'What if. . . .', which can either open up a disturbing possibility or dismiss an imagined objection as unimportant, is a way of suggesting two lines of thought in the same words, thus extending the scope of the questioning and sharpening our awareness of the appalling difficulty of arriving at any adequate response.

I have again referred to 'the speaker' rather than 'the poet'; but the next lines suggest that this speaker, whether or not he represents W. B. Yeats in his own person, is an Irish poet. To 'write it out in a verse' may seem a trivial act, an absurdly inadequate reaction to the events of Easter 1916; it suggests 'That is all I can do.' Yet it also represents a solemn act of commemorating the dead – the Irish poet accepting his responsibility to make a verbal monument – and, in this act, 'verse' evokes something of the supernatural powers attributed to rhymed and metrical incantation in the Celtic bardic tradition.

The poem ends, then, with those six powerful lines – very appropriate, we might think, for inscribing in stone or bronze, a monument in a public place. But this would not be so easy. The poem is written in quatrains in which alternate lines rhyme, and very often the sense of a sentence runs on from one quatrain into the next. If the rhyme is to preserved, we must take not six lines but eight – and that would break a question in half, making it unintelligible. To find a beginning point for our quotation, then, we would have to go back to the beginning of the fourth section, and include all that questioning – not at all appropriate for chiselling on stone. Yeats has shaped his poem to resist selective quotation; the whole poem must be the monument.

3 *Imagery and Rhythm*

> On a huge hill,
> Cragged and steep, Truth stands, and he that will
> Reach her, about must, and about must go;
> And what the hill's suddenness resists, win so.
>
> John Donne, *Satire III*

This chapter considers some of the ways in which words can say more than a dictionary and a grammar can account for. I shall use the word 'imagery' for all of them, although it usually has a narrower meaning. If, as I have suggested, poetry is to render accessible to readers the activity of a mind at work in pursuit of elusive truths, it needs all the resources the language affords. The use of some of these resources is illustrated in the poems that will be quoted and discussed. Regarded in this way, imagery will be considered primarily as functional – as means by which a poet communicates, extending and modifying meaning – rather than as decorative.

When Shakespeare's Othello, early in the play, is confronted by a hostile senator and his armed supporters, he says to them: 'Keep up your bright swords, for the dew will rust them.' He is not given this picturesque turn of speech in order to suggest that he has an endearing inclination to fanciful irrelevancies (or, what many people suppose to be the same thing, a poetic nature). The words that are not necessary to the command itself are there to clarify Othello's estimation of the danger, of the armed civilians who face him, and, by implication, of himself. He is a professional soldier, and *his* sword was not made for elegance: 'bright' suggests 'Yes, very pretty – now put them away.' This is extended by 'for the dew will rust them' – 'It would be a pity to make them dirty (not that they are likely to be stained by anything but dew).'

Before going on to examine another passage from a play, I must acknowledge the objection that plays are generally intended to be seen on the stage, not read in a book, and that during a performance, when one cannot go back to check possible cross-references, or stop to search for 'deeper meanings', anything that is not immediately apparent will be lost. But I think that if the play is well performed and attentively heard, ideas that are actively if unobtrusively present in the writing will in fact pass into the spectator's mind, without the dramatist, the producer, the actor or the spectator knowing just how the transfer has been effected. If this is so, we are sufficiently justified, once in a while, in taking a closer look at a part of a play and trying to see how it happens. This is what I shall now do with a passage from *The Revenger's Tragedy*, by Cyril Tourneur. It comes from Act 3 scene 4; the speaker, Vendice, addresses a skull which he carries in his hand.

And now methinks I could e'en chide myself
For doating on her beauty, though her death
Shall be revenged after no common action.
Does the silkworm expend her yellow labours
For thee? For thee does she undo herself?
Are lordships sold to maintain ladyships
For the poor benefit of a bewildering minute?
Why does yon fellow falsify highways,
And put his life between the judge's lips,
To refine such a thing – keeps horse and men
To beat their valours for her?

The first three lines introduce a meditation on a traditional theme, of which the best-known example is the graveyard scene in *Hamlet*, first performed about five years before Tourneur's play; the speech develops the idea expressed by Hamlet (who also holds a skull): 'Now get you to my lady's chamber, and tell her, let her paint an inch thick, to this favour she must come.'

'Yellow labours' is clearly not a construction allowed for in normal English usage, any more than Marvell's 'green thought in a green shade'. But it is quite readily intelligible: the imagined silkworm's coccoon is yellow. This is the first indication that the poet has 'realized' the image of the silkworm – made it real in his imagination, not just thought it up and put it there: he has imaginatively entered into the yellow world of the silk-worm's labours. And in the next line he compresses at least two imaginative perceptions in the word 'undo': the silkworm undoes herself in the sense of destroying herself; also, more fancifully (and unentomologically) she unwinds herself like a spool. I said 'at least two' because in its context we are likely to recognize behind the account of the silkworm the image of the woman who undoes herself with the same ambiguity: unbuttoning herself for her own destruction. The silkworm's self-destruction is for a lady – a lady seen, here, in the skull that is being addressed: 'for thee'. The exclamation is stressed both by its position at the beginning of a line, after a momentary hesitation, and by its immediate repetition, with increasing scorn. *She*, the stress implies, is not worth the exertions of a silkworm.

In the next line we have the false parallel (not a failure, for falsity is one of the things the passage is about) between 'lordships' – the estates of a lord, which could be sold in fact though hardly honourably since they were not mere possessions but responsibilities, stewardships – and 'ladyships', which are evidently not the estates of a lady but the lady herself, regarded mockingly: there goes her ladyship! Falsehood has not yet been mentioned, though it soon will be; but it is suggested in 'bewildering' – the consummation of this (not love but) bargain is not an ecstasy that resolves all perplexities, but on the contrary a climax of confusion.

The highwayman 'falsifies' highways by perverting them from their proper purpose – endangers communication in the state as, on a smaller scale, lying does in a personal relationship. The highwayman, like the silkworm, is imagined, not merely introduced as an idea. He is seen as putting his life 'between the judge's lips' – voluntarily placing his life in hazard: the phrase evokes the moment when the judge is about to pronounce sentence, and the convicted highwayman fixes his eyes on the judge's lips as if his life were really *there*, his fate depending on what words those lips would shape next. The line brings together two separate moments: the moment of choice, when by deciding to rob, the man placed his life in jeopardy, and the later moment when the consequence of that choice comes upon him, as risk turns into certainty.

All this is 'to refine such a thing': such a thing that is, we have by now been persuaded, incapable of refinement (the end-product of the refinement is, in any case, a skull); all her self-destroying lovers can do is give her finery, make her a fine ladyship. The horses and men employed by the highwayman 'beat their valours' – valour does not spark spontaneously for 'such a thing': it has to be whipped up, and is injured in the process.

Now each image in the passage has, I think, been adequately accounted for; and we are not far from being able to show why each word in the passage needs to be as it is. But something else is going on at the same time, something I have not yet mentioned at all. An image of gold runs through the whole passage; although it is never explicitly mentioned, its presence can be felt. It comes to mind, faintly at first, in the proximity of the words 'expend' and 'yellow': somewhere, behind the scenes, gold is being spent. Then we find 'sold', and 'poor benefit' meaning 'a poor return on investment'. And once the gold is sufficiently established in our minds – though always at the back of our minds – the image is kept alive in the momentary touches of 'refine' and 'beat'.

It is of course a merit in a poet (as in anybody else) to say what he means, and no merit to conceal his meaning. So why does this poet not mention gold, if only once, to make the reader or spectator fully conscious of it? Probably because concealment is part of his meaning: the relationship here described – that between a lady who trades on her beauty and her high-class clientele – is precisely one held together by money, but one in which money would not be mentioned. Both parties would be aware, all the time, of the payment of a price, but nothing so vulgar as gold would actually change hands, still less be mentioned. This is what the poetry enacts.

The conventional adjective of praise for imagery is 'vivid'. One thing that the passage I have just discussed has illustrated is that although imagery may be admirably vivid, it may also be admirably dim: the fact that it is only half perceived may be an important part of its meaning. Thus when Hamlet ponders

Whether 'tis nobler in the mind to suffer
The slings and arrows of outrageous fortune,
Or to take arms against a sea of troubles,
And by opposing end them,

the idea of taking arms against a sea is *not* made vivid: we hardly notice it, our attention being focused on the choice between endurance and active resistance. Yet it is sufficiently present to register the improbability of success, so that the apparent confidence of the concluding phrase 'And by opposing end them' is undermined. An active resistance to evils could not be convincingly undertaken without a determination to succeed: that is what is conveyed by the rhythmic force of 'And by opposing, end them.' But the simultaneous recognition that the enterprise is not a hopeful one, conveyed by 'take arms against a sea', is what makes it natural that Hamlet's thoughts move directly into a consideration of death as the likely outcome, for him, of such resistance.

It is a matter of common experience that the meaning of an utterance may be different from – may even be the reverse of – its literal or dictionary meaning. 'You astonish me', said with a certain intonation, can mean 'What you say is boringly obvious.' Although poetry is generally circulated in the form of printed words, it has to be recreated as spoken words by the reader, and there are various ways in which the printed text can indicate to the reader how it is to be spoken. Probably the simplest reason for writing plays in verse is to give the dramatist some control over how the actors speak the lines. Thus, it is part of the meaning of *Macbeth* that when Macbeth is told that his wife is dead he should say,

She should have died hereafter;
There would have been a time for such a word.
Tomorrow, and tomorrow, and tomorrow,
Creeps in this petty pace from day to day. . . .

and not, as he did in a recent production by the Royal Shakespeare Company:

She should have died hereafter;
There would have been a time for such a word tomorrow.
And tomorrow?
And tomorrow creeps in this petty pace from day to day. . . .

It is possible, of course, to resist in such ways the demands of the metre, but it can hardly be questioned that this involves a distortion of the meaning. When I refer to the rhythm or movement of a poem or a line, I mean the rhythm that results from a responsive reading of the text – a reading aloud, which seeks to reconcile the natural movement of the speaking voice with the demands of the metre. Consider, for example, this poem by Andrew Marvell:

To His Coy Mistress

Had we but world enough, and time,
This coyness, Lady, were no crime.
We would sit down and think which way
To walk and pass our long love's day.
Thou by the Indian Ganges' side
Shouldst rubies find: I by the tide
Of Humber would complain. I would
Love you ten years before the Flood,
And you should, if you please, refuse
Till the conversion of the Jews.
My vegetable love should grow
Vaster than empires, and more slow;
An hundred years should go to praise
Thine eyes and on thy forehead gaze;
Two hundred to adore each breast;
But thirty thousand to the rest;
An age at least to every part,
And the last age should show your heart;
For, Lady, you deserve this state,
Nor would I love at lower rate.

But at my back I always hear
Time's wingèd chariot hurrying near;
And yonder all before us lie
Deserts of vast eternity.
Thy beauty shall no more be found,
Nor, in thy marble vault, shall sound
My echoing song: then worms shall try
That long preserved virginity,
And your quaint honour turn to dust,
And into ashes all my lust:
The grave's a fine and private place,
But none, I think, do there embrace.

Now therefore, while the youthful hue
Sits on thy skin like morning dew,
And while thy willing soul transpires
At every pore with instant fires,
Now let us sport us while we may,
And now, like amorous birds of prey,
Rather at once our time devour
Than languish in his slow-chapt power.
Let us roll all our strength and all
Our sweetness up into one ball,
And tear our pleasures with rough strife
Thorough the iron gates of life:
Thus, though we cannot make our sun
Stand still, yet we will make him run.

To say that this poem is written in iambic tetrameters – or, more intelligibly, in lines of eight syllables, with stressed and unstressed syllables alternating, the first being unstressed – is not to say that every line conforms with this description. (In the first section, only two lines do). Rather, it means that each line in some degree approximates to this pattern, so that we very soon recognize in reading the poem that this, rather than another, is the pattern to which the lines approximate and from which they significantly diverge.

The first line evidently starts with a stressed monosyllable, its stress perhaps made more emphatic by the fact that it is a divergence from the metrical pattern. And it needs this special stress because it is a key word in the argument, like the openings of the other sections. For the poem has, in paraphrase, a simple and lucid argument; it could be summarized like this: '*If* we had unlimited time, nothing would please me better than to court you without haste. *But* our time is limited by the inescapable fact of death. *Therefore* (unfortunately) we must hurry, and love urgently if we are to love at all.' Rhythm and meaning are interdependent, and finally inseparable; it is in understanding the meaning of the opening couplet that we decide that 'no' requires a full stress, equal to that of 'crime', again resisting the metrical expectation that it should be unstressed.

But while the speaking voice responds to the primary need to 'make sense' of the words on the page, it will at the same time acknowledge the metre – it will not read the verse as if it were prose. The next six lines of the poem invite a reading that is not a metrical jog-trot, but is also significantly different from

We would sit down, and think which way to walk and pass our long love's day. Thou by the Indian Ganges' side shouldst rubies find; I by the tide of Humber would complain. I would love you ten years before the flood. . . .

Without making a pause after 'way' (for that would not make sense), we must find a reading that will acknowledge the line-ending. Probably the outcome will be a slight but perceptible lingering on 'way', and in the act of speaking it we find that we are being led by the verse to enact its meaning – which is about lingering. In similar ways the other statements in the first section that run on across line-endings invite a hesitating, lei-surely movement of the voice, so that the act of reading is an imitation of the pace that is described. Other features con-tribute to the same effect: 'vegetable' is a surprising word, and can not be hurried over; the long syllable of 'Vaster' at the beginning of a line slows the movement; the words 'least to' are hard to make fully distinct from each other and require a momentary separation, and in the following line the words 'age should' more insistently demand a little space between them. After such impediments, the closing couplet

For, Lady, you deserve this state,
Nor would I love at lower rate

are easy to say, and from the rhetorical weight of

And the last age should show your heart

the voice drops to a more relaxed, conversational tone.

In the second section the opening words introduce a startling 'ratatatat' rhythm, making a decisive break from both the slow-ness and the relaxation that preceded them. This is the 'But' section of the argument, showing why the paradisal prolon-gation of invitation and refusal will not do. The speaking voice encountering a metrical difficulty in the second line – where 'chariot hurrying' takes longer to say than the four normal syllables that the metre allows for – can not, in this section, take its time; the meaning determines its response, which is to hurry and try to fit the words into the line – the line now experienced as an allotted span of time into which much must be crammed. This hasty scramble is soon over, and the next couplet presents ironically a prospect of an unhurried future – not 'world enough, and time' but the endless absence of both after death: 'Deserts of vast eternity.' (In the seventeenth century the line would have sounded more like 'Desarts of vast etarnity', with three similar long vowels adding a sound-image of monotony.) The difficulty of carrying the sense across the line division in

Nor, in thy marble vault, shall sound
My echoing song

causes the voice to dwell on 'sound' and draws attention to its being a rhyming (echoing) word. We can hardly speak the lines without pondering the sound of 'sound'; and this pondering is at the same time required by the form of the negative statement, which says not only that the lover's song will not sound in the lady's tomb, but also that if it did, it would echo: the poet has imagined the improbable act and leads the reader to do so too. The macabre physicality of the foreseen posthumous seduction, in which worms attempt the penetration denied to the lover, is realized in the act of speaking 'try', syntactically unresolved at the end of the line. The eminently tidy resolution, in the following couplet, of honour and lust into dust and ashes, is a contrasting way of emphasizing that both the conflict and its significance will be over. The closing couplet, like that of the first section, drops to a more colloquial register, with 'I think' helping to define the tone of sardonic understatement.

In the summarized argument of the poem, as I suggested earlier, the last section presents an unfortunate makeshift that we have to put up with because we can not have 'world enough, and time' for the unhurried courtship of the first section. Yet in fact the last section is not experienced in that way; the repetition of 'Now', strongly stressed three times, demands a reading that registers not only the urgency that the argument requires, but also an eagerness that is rather different – a positive delight that goes with the vividly presented appreciation of the most transient features of the lady's beauty. There is delight too in the ferocity of the defiance of time, the determination to consume time instead of passively being consumed by it. Looking back now to the opening section, we are better able to assess its tone in relation to the range of tones given by the whole poem, and to recognize a certain wilful absurdity in its representation of ideal human love on such an inhuman time-scale. It may be inappropriate to visualize 'My vegetable love' as a monstrously overgrown cabbage, but there is certainly no anachronism in seeing the implication that such a love, however vast, would be inferior in kind to animal love, let alone ideal human love. On re-reading, we may also find that 'Nor would I love at lower rate' suggests, with its mercantile vocabulary, a sardonic comment on the lady's thinking that a prompt acquiescence would reduce the value of the love. On the other hand, the last section, which seems explicitly to be offering a second-best, an unwelcome but sadly necessary haste, is really proposing a love that we recognize as far richer, more intense, and more fully human: the unsparing confrontation of the reality of death in the second section is the foundation on which Marvell constructs the vividness and joy of the third.

Marvell, along with Donne, Herbert and some other seventeenth-century poets, is often called a *metaphysical* poet. The description has an interesting history; it was first applied by Samuel Johnson as a derogatory term to a kind of poetry that he considered over-ingenious. 'The metaphysical poets', he wrote in his *Life of Cowley*, 'were men of learning, and to show their learning was their whole endeavour. . . . The most heterogeneous ideas are yoked by violence together; nature and art are ransacked for illustrations, comparisons, and allusions.' In the first decades of the present century there was a renewal of interest in, and appreciation of, these poets, and the strenuousness of their thought came to be seen as wholly compatible with emotion deeply felt. The term *metaphysical* continued, and continues, to be applied to these poets, but its use no longer implies any judgement of the quality of their poetry.

But the final couplet of *To His Coy Mistress* entitles the poem to be called a metaphysical poem not only in this general and rather loose sense, but in the more strict sense that it is a poem that deals with one of the fundamental philosophical problems – the nature of time, and how human life and experience relate to it. It is the whole poem – irony, pace and all – that gives meaning to the concluding proposition that there is, after all, a sense in which one *can* master time and change;

Thus, though we cannot make our sun
Stand still, yet we will make him run.

I have heard that the harpsichordist Wanda Landowska was
once asked how sure she could be that her performances of
Bach were as the composer had intended. She replied, 'If Bach
were to appear now and say "That is not how I meant my work
to be played," I would answer: "Go back to sleep, Mr Bach; you
have done your part; this is my part." ' A poem, like a musical
composition, is not a group of marks on paper, but an experience recreated by following – as carefully, intelligently, and
imaginatively as one can – the indications given by the printed
notation. Probably no two readers will read a poem in quite the
same way; certainly the poem will sound different read by a
Yorkshire and a Kentish speaker; yet, if each is duly responsive
both to the text and to his or her own normal speech, it will be
recognizably the same poem. It will not, of course, be the same
poem if some idiosyncratic affectation of speech is imposed on
it; I suspect that very few poems could survive the curious man-
nerism of radio commentators who stress all prepositions ('Now
let's go over TO John Smutch IN Washington. John, what IN
your opinion will be the reaction OF the U.S. TO the discussion
OF these issues BY the Security Council IN the next few days?')
And I have already mentioned how actors can sometimes
destroy the movement and meaning of the lines they speak. But
in discussing the relations established between the speaking
voice and the metre and meaning of a poem, I am not talking
about professional speakers but about 'common readers'
trying, in their reading, to respond appropriately to the words
on the page.

   The comments I made on *To His Coy Mistress* will have suggested that the poem needs to be read aloud, and that its
meaning emerges partly from the experience of this activity.
Hearing it read aloud, or imagining the sound while reading
silently, is not enough without experiencing the various kinds
of ease and difficulty, the various kinds of decision, involved in
producing the spoken poem. In this effort to recreate as far as
we can the whole meaning of a poem, differences of pronunciation are not very important: Wordsworth's poems seem to be
fully accessible to southern readers, and we do not have to fake
an Irish pronunciation in reading Yeats. Nor does it seem very

important that poems written in earlier centuries were at first spoken with pronunciations different from our own, whatever those may be; we can still distinguish quite subtle nuances of meaning in Shakespeare's poetry, and if (as some reconstructions suggest) Shakespeare's earliest actors sounded rather like Ulstermen domiciled in Devonshire, that was their problem: we have ours, and only occasionally are these affected by facts or conjectures about Shakespeare's pronunciation. For us to try to imitate it would make the poetry sound very odd, and there is no reason to suppose that it sounded at all odd to its earliest audiences.

When we go further back, to medieval poetry, we may well encounter some difficulty. Often a modern pronunciation will fail to make sense of rhythms and rhymes, and only after some practice can we adapt our pronunciation of familiar words and find appropriate pronunciations for unfamiliar ones. But our primary concern is still, it seems to me, to make sense of the poem rather than to try to make it sound as it might have sounded in the fourteenth or thirteenth century.

Consider, for example, the anonymous medieval lyric *I sing of a maiden* (a *lyric* is simply a series of stanzas that were, or sound as if they were, composed to be sung):

I sing of a maiden
That is makeles:
King of alle kinges
To here sone she ches.

He cam also stille
Ther his moder was,
As dew in Aprille
That falleth on the grass.

He cam also stille
To his moderes bowr,
As dew in Aprille
That falleth on the flowr.

He cam also stille
Ther his moder lay
As dew in Aprille
That falleth on the spray.

Moder and maiden
Was never non but she:
Well may swich a lady
Godes moder is.

The words 'ches' at the end of the first stanza is an obsolete
form of 'chose'. 'Makeles' in line 2 is more difficult; from its basic
sense of 'without a companion' we can reasonably suppose its
primary meaning to be either 'matchless' or 'unmated' – with
the other present as a secondary meaning; and there is also, I
think, in the combined presence of these meanings and of the
sound of the word, a suggestion of 'immaculate'.

One of the first things one notices about this poem is its shape:
the repetition, with variations, in stanzas 2, 3 and 4. And this
repetition seems to increase the stillness, the quietness, rather
as if, for fear of disturbing the blessed lady, or of making any
noise in such a holy place, the speaker (or singer) hardly dares
do more than repeat – as if to say a new or different thing might
jar. In these three stanzas the voice seems to be very much
under the spell of the event, attentive to it – and drawing our
attention to it – with no more than a whispered comment; each
of these stanzas seems more hushed than the one before it.
What is enacted is the quietness of awe in the presence of a
miracle, a sacred mystery. For this we have been prepared by
the first stanza, where the maiden is said to have chosen the
King of Kings for her son: and a certain simple matter-of-fact-
ness in the statement does not conceal – rather, it empha-
sizes – the uniqueness of choosing a son (while common
humanity may choose a husband or wife, but takes what it gets
in the way of sons).

But when we have observed the effect of repetition in stanzas
2, 3 and 4, we have yet to consider the effect of the variations,
which are, in fact, made to stand out by their very slightness.
The stillness is constant, though one's sense of it increases with
the repetition: the falling dew is just as much a measure of
soundlessness whatever it falls on – even if it fell on a rock it
would not audibly clatter. So the grass, the flower and the spray
are not, as far as the bare analogy is concerned, significant;
they are decorations. But perhaps we would do better to call
them, like the marginal pictures in medieval manuscripts, *illu-
minations*. For they do add something to the meaning; and
there is a progression from one to the next. First the grass, a

horizontal expanse; then the solitary flower rising out of it; then the spray, the cluster of flowers and foliage. It suggests a cinematic sequence, and the flower, and then the spray, have appeared as if from nowhere. And now it is clear that 'April' is there not because the dew of July or October would be noisier, but because April is the month of birth and growth in nature.

As for the other variation –

Ther his moder was
To his moderes bowr
Ther his moder lay

– I suppose I could not convincingly deny that it may have been accidental: that is, introduced merely to provide the necessary rhymes for the other, and more important, variation. But if it was an accident, it was a singularly felicitous one. In stanza 2 the maiden merely 'was', somewhere; in stanza 3 she is localized; in 4 she is seen to be lying. The movement of the narration closer to the object, with increasing concentration on, and clarity of perception of, the centre of attention, is much older than the cinema; it is an imitation of a characteristic activity of the attentive eye. (There is an impressive example in the opening lines of *Sir Gawain*.)

The conclusion of the poem is not a logical outcome of any argument. But it does emerge, with its own kind of logic, from the tenderness and reverence which the rest of the poem has enacted. Emerging in this way, it is not a controversial theological statement. To read it as such would be to misread the tone and nature of the poem, which is just as radical a misunderstanding as a misreading of the literal content would be. If, in the process of responding to the poem – that is, recreating the poem ourselves – we come to

Wel may swich a lady
Godes moder be

and find ourselves saying 'Yes' to it, this 'Yes' does not commit us to a dogma, nor indeed to any judgement, even a momentary one, on a matter of theological or historical fact. Rather, it expresses our recognition of the validity of an experience, an experience in which we have participated by recreating it. So it need not make much difference to our reading of the poem whether we are, or consider ourselves to be, Calvinists or Catholics or Agnostics or Mormons; for it is not a matter of agreeing or disagreeing with the poem. One doesn't agree or disagree with the sun shining on snow, or with the rumble of distant thunder. Like those, the poem is an experience. And if, ten minutes after participating richly in this experience, we should find it necessary to argue, in a different kind of discussion, that mariolatry is a popish superstition that debases the human intellect, we shall at least have a better notion of what we are talking about than if we had not, in reading this poem, experienced an honest moment of adoration of the Blessed Virgin.

We have seen how metrical poems can control the movement of the speaking voice in ways that extend the meanings of the words. It is less easy to show how poems in free verse do this, where there is no regular metrical pattern or stanza form to establish a set of expectations. Even prose, of course, has punctuation to give some measure of control over the rhythms of speech; and free verse has, in addition, line divisions to indicate rhythmical groupings which may coincide with or modify those suggested by the punctuation. Often, too, we may recognize, in free verse, passages or single lines that fall into patterns familiar to us from our experience of metrical verse. But from line to line we do not know what to expect; and the reader of free verse needs to practise rather different kinds of alertness from those required by metrical verse.

An excerpt from D. H. Lawrence's poem *Kangaroo* will illustrate this.

Her little loose hands, and drooping Victorian shoulders.
And then her great weight below the waist, her vast pale belly
With a thin young yellow little paw hanging out, and straggle
                    of a long thin ear, like ribbon,
Like a funny trimming to the middle of her belly, thin little
                    dangle of an immature paw, and one thin ear.
Her belly, her big haunches
And in addition, the great muscular python-stretch of her tail.

The first line is divided by a comma, and it is clear that the two parts are rhythmically contrasting, their relative quickness and slowness matching the relative lightness and weight of the kangaroo's 'hands' and 'shoulders'. In the first part it is the word 'little' that sets the pace; in the second, the similarity of the three long stressed syllables retards the speaking voice. The contrast is not very marked, but it introduces the more striking difference of pace between the second line and the two that follow. The succession of two long stressed syllables in 'great weight' cannot be ignored, because they rhyme with each other; the voice must linger here. Then the same long vowel occurs again, in 'waist', linked alliteratively with 'weight'. The 'st' at the end of 'waist' is taken up again at the end of the emphatic monosyllable 'vast' – which is the first of a series of three consecutive stressed syllables. A responsive reading voice will necessarily dwell on these words, acknowledging the emphasis they gain from these links of rhyme, alliteration and assonance – giving them, that is, a certain 'weight'. In contrast, the two lines that follow fall easily into quick, light rhythms, so unexpectedly metrical in their effect that it seems almost appropriate to beat time to them while reading. Again, and more strikingly than in the first line, the contrasting movements communicate a difference between weight and lightness – here the difference of scale between the mother kangaroo and the young one in its pouch. The next short line returns to the adult kangaroo, and the last line adds an impression of its tail in words that require in the speaking a muscular force that is itself part of the communication. What the whole excerpt conveys is not just a 'picture' of the kangaroo, but a sense of it – of its size, weight and energy. The reader's discovery of the rhythms, in the process of speaking, is what makes the words more communicative than their dictionary meanings.

If the word 'imagery' is taken to mean, as I suggested at the beginning of this chapter, all the ways in which words can say more than a dictionary and a grammar can account for, it seems by now that rhythm must be included by it – at least when it is used expressively rather than decoratively. But readers may well baulk at this attempt to have a word mean what I want it to mean, and I shall not insist on it. Perhaps it is enough to have planted a little doubt about where the line should be drawn, if it can be drawn at all, between imagery and rhythm.

Several kinds of imagery are conveniently exhibited in the next poem, *The Habit of Perfection* by Gerard Manley Hopkins. It is not one of his great ones, but still, I think, an impressive achievement.

Elected Silence, sing to me
And beat upon my whorlèd ear,
Pipe me to pastures still and be
The music that I care to hear.

Shape nothing, lips; be lovely-dumb:
It is the shut, the curfew sent
From there where all surrenders come
Which only makes you eloquent.

Be shellèd, eyes, with double dark
And find the uncreated light:
This ruck and reel which you remark
Coils, keeps, and teases simple sight.

Palate, the hutch of tasty lust,
Desire not to be rinsed with wine:
The can must be so sweet, the crust
So fresh that come in fasts divine!

Nostrils, your careless breath that spend
Upon the stir and keep of pride,
What relish shall the censers send
Along the sanctuary side!

O feel-of-primrose hands, O feet
That want the yield of plushy sward,
But you shall walk the golden street
And you unhouse and house the Lord.

And, Poverty, be thou the bride
And now the marriage feast begun,
And lily-coloured clothes provide
Your spouse not laboured-at or spun.

The poem enacts an imagined decision to enter a monastic order of extreme austerity – enclosed, and under vows of poverty and silence. It seems likely that the poem was related to Hopkins' decision to become a priest of the Roman Catholic church, but it is not simply autobiographical. In the poem, the imagined postulant tries to persuade his senses, which he loves, to accept their various renunciations, and promises them compensations, not purely spiritual, but appropriate to each of the organs he addresses.

'Whorlèd ear' seems to me to be primarily visual, though not without an evocation of the sense of touch. The conformations of both the outer and the inner ear are suggested; and the 'ear', which would otherwise have been merely a part of a cliché ('beat upon my ear'), becomes a real, visible, tangible and loved ear. The silence that the speaker invokes is 'elected', not the involuntary and constricting silence of deafness, but his own chosen silence, and (given the theological associations of 'elect') God's silence. It is this that he asks to lead him, and God becomes the good shepherd of the twenty-third Psalm with the compressed allusion to 'green pastures' and 'still waters'. – Yet not quite that Jehovah of the Old Testament, who doesn't, I think, play the pipes. He merges, here, into the shepherds of classical pastoral poetry, and is delicately endowed with the rather un-Jehovah-like gaiety of the great god Pan. The elected silence is not yet the music that the speaker cares to hear: he asks it to become so; but he speaks of the silence in such a singing line that one must believe it to be delightful to him already.

In the second stanza the painful associations of 'dumb' are cancelled, though not without some tension, by the hyphenated 'lovely'; so that we come upon the word 'dumb' from an unaccustomed direction, and are drawn to consider it freshly. It leaves the mouth closed at the end of the line, with a pause – long enough to savour this dumbness in our imagination. But though lovely, it is a 'shut': here we have a foretaste of Hopkins' later violence with language – his contempt for mere decorum and 'poetical' convention. The 'shut' is rough, uncouth, ungentle, utterly final. The curfew is the putting out of fires – here, of course, eloquence – the eloquence of the world, as opposed to what the last line of the stanza offers as true eloquence.

The eyes are to be 'shellèd' – covered by the eyelids as by shells – which suggests the shape of the eyelids as well as making them more absolutely opaque, while the unwanted association of shells with stony hardness is opposed by the lingering on *ll* in the word. I have suggested that the poem is not a great one: there is, after all, something rather mechanical in this manipulation of imagery; and there are moments of obscurity that give us reason to suspect unsureness in the writing. 'Double dark' seems to be one such obscurity. It may merely be the darkness of two eyes closed; but since one eye closed brings no darkness at all, this reading is unsatisfactory. Or it may mean that both light in its literal sense, and the light of human reason, are to be renounced; but this is not indicated clearly enough to be fully communicative, and anyway a total renunciation of human reason (as distinct from a readiness to suspend it or transcend it in the contemplation of the mysteries of the faith) would be theologically reprehensible. In any case, the renunciation of the light created when God said 'Let there be light' is to be made in order that the light that *is* God may be found. When the eyes are open, the confusion of the visible world (an untidy heap, 'ruck', in a state of violent and apparently disorderly movement, 'reel') traps the attention, holds it back from the invisible realities, and 'teases' perhaps by continually inducing in us the illusion that with a little more perseverance we shall be able to see what it is all about. Again such words as 'ruck' and 'reel' are used to give a roughness, a brutal force, to the vision of the world that is to be renounced.

In the next stanza it is the word 'hutch' that is both the surprise and the centre of force: the stanza would be far less remarkable without it. 'Lust' here is fairly general, since it is taken to mean, principally, excessive delight in eating and drinking; we might read it as the delights of the flesh in general. 'Hutch', of course, suggests a rabbit: emblem of unbridled and impressive sexual performance, like the sparrow in earlier times. The mouth then, as the location of voluptuous tasting and kissing, is turned into the home of a rather smelly and disreputable animal (though cuddly). But there still remains something to be accounted for in the strange effectiveness of the word 'hutch'. It is not the sound of it so much as the physical sensation of saying it that enriches the meaning. To say the line is to become vividly aware of the palate – and not merely visually through the suggestion of a box-like shape. What happens is that with the *l*s and *t*s and *s*s, the tongue caresses the palate, sometimes lingeringly, sometimes quickly on tiptongue: and in the middle of the line, just once, almost convulsively, voluptuously, presses itself against the palate. The suggestion of a place not wholly clean and sweet is taken up in the word 'rinsed', which also, of course, suggests the leisurely and discriminating savouring of an appreciated wine. What *will* rinse the palate, the stanza goes on to suggest, is the water and bread of fasting, the 'can' and the 'crust'. These are presented as sufficient compensations for the deprived palate, with the reminder that water may be sweet, and that a crust – which isolated at the end of the line suggests something hard and dry – is a very different diet if (as we discover in the next line after a moment's suspense) it is 'fresh'.

In the next stanza I can offer no satisfactory account of 'the stir and keep of pride'. In breathing, the air is stirred and retained; but there is nothing proud about this. The nostrils, where sneers take place, can well be associated with pride; and 'keep' might be a tower of a fortress, but 'stir' seems not to bear a meaning that would match this.

The 'feel-of-primrose hands' are at the same time soft and delicate hands, and hands accustomed to delight in soft and delicate textures. And 'the yield of plushy sward' makes real, in ways that I need not analyse, what it talks about.

The final stanza alludes to the Sermon on the Mount: 'Consider the lilies of the field, how they grow; they toil not, neither do they spin: and yet I say unto you, that even Solomon in all his glory was not arrayed like one of these.' But it is clumsily done, and the stanza is a weak and disappointing conclusion to a poem that begins with such concentration of meaning.

4 Meaning

And therefore though it be ever lawfull, and often times very usefull, for the raising and exaltation of our devotion, . . . to induce the *diverse senses* that the Scriptures doe admit, yet this may not be admitted, if there may be danger thereby, to neglect or weaken the *literall sense* it selfe. For there is no necessity of that *spirituall wantonnesse* of finding more then necessary senses; for, the more *lights* there are, the more *shadows* are also cast by those many lights. . . . When you have the *necessary sense*, that is the meaning of the holy Ghost in that place, you have senses enow, and not till then, though you have never so many, and never so delightfull.

John Donne, *Sermon preached at St Paul's, Christmas Day 1621*

This title is no more exclusive than 'Imagery and Rhythm'; for it could cover nearly everything that can be said about poetry. But it may serve to focus our attention, while we consider a number of poems, on some kinds of difficulty that we encounter in trying to understand what a poem is saying.

I have already shown that the meaning of a poem cannot be limited to its literal or paraphrasable content: that in Marvell's *To His Coy Mistress*, for example, the meaning of the poem contradicts the argument that a paraphrase would derive from it; and that imagery and rhythm, through which we experience the vehemence or hesitancy, gravity or lightness, of the utterance, can extend or modify the literal meaning and tell us how to take it – rather as, in conversation, tones of voice and facial expression may indicate to us that what is being said is being said ironically.

The meaning of a poem is not, then, one element in it that can be separated from the rest – what it says is not separable from how it says it. To say it in other words would be to say a different thing. This would seem to deny the possibility of giving an account of what we take a poem to mean, and so to deny the possibility of discussing a poem's meaning and even of finding out whether we agree or disagree about it.

Certainly it means that no account or interpretation can be an equivalent for the poem itself, reproduce its meaning in different terms, so as to replace the poem. What an interpretation can do, without any such perverse aspiration, is to draw attention to features of the poem that might be overlooked, to point out connections between them, to suggest ways of 'taking' the poem and its parts. It is an invitation to look again at the poem, to verify whether, read in the way suggested, it makes better sense, means more than one had realized.

In exploring my next example, a poem by Wallace Stevens, I shall outline a process (not *the* process, for many others are possible) by which a reader, or a group of readers in discussion, might arrive at a sense of the poem's meaning. It is a process of attending to the poem as a whole and to its parts; for the whole can be understood only as a result of understanding the parts, each of which can be understood only in the context of the whole.

A Dish of Peaches in Russia

With my whole body I taste these peaches,
I touch them and smell them. Who speaks?

I absorb them as the Angevine
Absorbs Anjou. I see them as a lover sees,

As a young lover sees the first buds of spring
And as the black Spaniard plays his guitar.

Who speaks? But it must be that I,
That animal, that Russian, that exile, for whom

The bells of the chapel pullulate sounds at
Heart. The peaches are large and round,

Ah! and red; and they have peach fuzz, ah!
They are full of juice and the skin is soft.

They are full of the colors of my village
And of fair weather, summer, dew, peace.

The room is quiet where they are.
The windows are open. The sunlight fills

The curtains. Even the drifting of the curtains,
Slight as it is, disturbs me. I did not know

That such ferocities could tear
One self from another, as these peaches do.

There can be no doubt that the poem is about an intense
awareness of peaches – the taste, touch and smell of peaches,
their size, shape, colour and texture. This vivid awareness
extends to the associations of peaches: they evoke for the
speaker a sense of the familiar and of the affectionately
remembered – a rich sense of home, of 'my village'.

So far there is no problem, except that the intensity of experience seems rather excessive for a dish of peaches; but
perhaps we ought to value this as an example of the way in
which a poem, like a painting, can make familiar objects,
usually taken for granted, excitingly fresh and strange. But so
far I have avoided what is really hard to understand in the
poem, and have offered no account of the repeated question
'Who speaks?', nor of the puzzling fourth stanza, nor of the final
sentence.

With the first 'Who speaks?', we may register an ambiguity: it
may mean 'Did somebody interrupt me?', or it may mean 'Was
it I, or someone else, who spoke these words?' With the repetition of the question, followed by 'But it must be that I', it
becomes clear that the speaker is referring to the words present
in the poem; we may now dismiss the first of the two inter-
pretations that had seemed possible. But the speaker now
seems to be (and to have been in the first stanza) expressing
astonishment that *he* should have spoken of the peaches as he
has: it is as if it is not his customary self that has spoken, but
another self, an unfamiliar self, whom he has difficulty in recognizing and acknowledging.

It is 'a dish of peaches in Russia' that has evoked this
unfamiliar self, whom the speaker now identifies as 'that
Russian'; 'it must be' a Russian, for he responds to the Russian
peaches as one responds to one's home and its characteristic
and familiar features ('as the Angevine Absorbs Anjou', 'as the
black Spaniard plays his guitar').

In re-reading the poem at this stage we may very reasonably
have in mind a hypothetical interpretation, to be tested in the
reading, that takes the speaker in the poem to be a Russian,

who has lived so long in exile that he has almost forgotten his origin; the sight of a dish of peaches, taking him unawares, takes him back, by the evocative power of its operation on his senses, to the Russia that he remembers. For many years he has been accustomed to see himself as, perhaps, an American; and the effect of the peaches upon him startles him so that he hardly recognizes himself: 'Who speaks?' then means something like 'Surely it was not I who said that?' But the effect is too persistent to be denied, and when he asks the question a second time he has to acknowledge that 'that Russian' is in fact himself. He allows the peaches, and the reminiscences that they evoke, to carry him back, returning to 'my village', and then to what seems to be a specific remembered place, time and mood:

The room is quiet where they are.
The windows are open. The sunlight fills

The curtains. Even the drifting of the curtains,
Slight as it is, disturbs me.

The final sentence then makes perfectly satisfactory sense: the effect of the peaches is deeply disturbing to the speaker, who has gradually built up an identity in his second homeland, but finds himself irresistibly drawn back into an identity he has long since turned his back on.

But we come back to the fact that the peaches are 'in Russia'. Has the exile then returned, and seen the peaches there? If that were so, we could hardly imagine him to be so taken by surprise by something that reminds him of his Russian origin. Besides, 'The room is quiet where they are' may suggest (though not necessarily) that he is *not* there; and once we begin to entertain the possibility that he is not where the peaches are – that they are in Russia while he is in another country – we find some measure of confirmation that they are not visibly present to him in the fact (which perhaps we ought to have noticed earlier) that the sequence of sense-impressions is curious: *seeing* comes late, after tasting, touching and smelling. Only half way through the poem are the peaches *seen* to be 'large and round', and only then comes what sounds like a new discovery – 'Ah! and red; and they have peach fuzz, ah!' These would be one's first perceptions of things visibly present. Pondering the order in which the sense-impressions are given in the poem, don't we find it to be an accurate representation of the effect of hearing someone mention peaches? Or of coming upon a reference to a dish of peaches in a novel? If it should be a Russian novel, and its reader (the speaker in the poem) is not in Russia, would that fit the poem?

I think it would, and that on that basis we can make good sense of the poem. We might leave our puzzling at this point, and find the poem richly significant – an account of how a simple object, casually mentioned in a book one reads, may transport one back to a forgotten moment in the past, a closed period of one's life.

But something still seems not quite right. For a start, if that Russian exile were reading a Russian novel (even in English), he would hardly be so surprised to be reminded that he was a Russian; he would already be engaged in an activity that would not allow him to forget it. Then, if the two occurrences of 'Who speaks?' are taken to suggest some kind of parallel between the statements that occasion them, and if the first is occasioned by something like 'I experience these peaches as if they were physically present (but they are not)', then we may suppose the second to be occasioned by something like 'I experience these peaches in Russia as if I were a Russian (but I am not)'.

So we might arrive at another reading of the poem – a variant on the previous one. The speaker is not a Russian: he is, like us, an English-speaking reader, who encounters, perhaps in a Russian novel, the mention of a dish of peaches. The fulness of his response is as if he were a Russian exile – as if these peaches were familiar things that evoked memories of his homeland. At first the speaker can hardly admit that it is he who experiences them thus; his own words take him by surprise; he doubts whether he could have spoken them – 'Who speaks?' Then, reluctantly, he acknowledges that it is some part of himself, 'that I', that responds as if he were a Russian – reluctantly because he does not entirely approve of 'that I, that animal' and would prefer not to believe in his existence – 'But it must be.' Carried on by the associations of the peaches (associations perhaps themselves created by Russian novels) he allows them to evoke his imagined village, an imagined room, and finally his imagined mood described in a sentence that has a Chekhovian quality:

> Even the drifting of the curtains,
> Slight as it is, disturbs me.

Read in this way, I think the poem is fully effective. It explores the sense that many of us have, in reading Tolstoy or Chekhov, that ordinary details of everyday life in their fiction are often astonishingly un-foreign, surprisingly more familiar to us as English-speaking readers than corresponding details in French or German fiction. Whether this results from the quite exceptional skills of these Russian writers in creating for us the world of their fiction, so that we are made to become more familiar with it than we realize, or whether it is to be accounted for by long-standing cultural connections between Russia and England (especially the widespread knowledge of Shakespeare and Dickens in Russia), it is a common experience that English-speaking readers feel 'at home' in the fiction of pre-revolutionary Russia. The poem presents a person who feels this as if he had another self, brought startlingly into being by the chance detail of a dish of peaches in a book; and, read thus, it fully justifies the paradoxical attribution of 'ferocities' to such soft and unaggressive things as peaches.

Such a poem as I have been discussing is likely to present some difficulty to any reader; one has to struggle with the sense of it before one can usefully comment on its methods, and any critic's account of the poem would, fairly obviously, have to include an outline of what he takes it to mean. But with a less obviously puzzling poem, a critic will often assume that its meaning is obvious, and proceed at once to discuss whatever features of the poem are relevant to his argument without indicating what he takes it to be about. There are dangers in this; for the reader may suppose it to be about something quite different.

In an article on 'The Colloquial Mode of Byron' (in *Scrutiny*, volume XVI, no. 1), Marius Bewley quotes, to illustrate part of his argument, a poem by Richard Lovelace: *La Bella Bona-Roba*. (It is doubtful whether this title really belongs to the poem – see C. H. Wilkinson, *The Poems of Richard Lovelace*, Oxford 1930.)

I cannot tell who loves the skeleton
Of a poor marmoset, naught but bone, bone.
Give me a nakedness with her clothes on.

Such whose white-satin upper coat of skin,
Cut upon velvet rich incarnadin,
Has yet a body (and of flesh) within.

Sure it is meant good husbandry in men,
Who do incorporate with aery lean,
T' repair their sides, and get their rib again.

Hard hap unto the huntsman that decrees
Fat joys for all his sweat, whenas he sees
After his 'say, naught but his keeper's fees.

Then Love I beg, when next thou tak'st thy bow,
Thy angry shafts, and dost heart-chasing go,
Pass rascal deer, strike me the largest doe.

He comments on the poem's 'deceptive modernity', draws attention to 'the reflective repetition of "bone" in Stanza I', and observes that 'the singularity of the opening figure, "skeleton of a poor marmoset", has a strangeness that is acceptable at once because it is so profoundly personal'. He goes on to say:

In the second, third, and fourth stanzas the rhythm continues to mirror the activity of the working mind with considerable subtlety, and the terse directness, the 'colloquial' spareness, of many of the words is effective. Several of the figures are of a somewhat homely variety, but woven with sureness into the courtly fabric. Thus, 'Fat joys for all his sweat', 'T' repair their sides', and 'keeper's fees' look back to the best imagery in Jacobean dramatic writing. These middle stanzas are certainly colloquial if one is permitted to define 'colloquial' as an effective, familiarly free gallantry of language with its own syntactical and decorous proprieties. But with Stanza 5 the real reason for taking this poem of Lovelace's as a good example of the point to be made becomes apparent. Stanza 5 represents a decided shift in imagery. The sinuosities of personal thought are here ironed out in a highly conventional development. But Stanza 2, one now recognizes, had represented an anticipation of this conventional resolution, and in Stanza 5 one has the delicious recognition that one has already been prepared for this change in tone.

It would be hard to pick out any comment to disagree with here, or to say at what point I began to wonder whether the critic was not taking the poem to mean something quite different from what I thought it meant: whether, in effect, he was not commenting on a different poem from the one I was reading. At any rate it can not be clear how 'the rhythm continues to mirror the activity of the working mind' if writer and reader do not know that they agree what activity the working mind is engaged in.

A later issue of the journal (volume XVI, no. 3) published a letter from a reader, disagreeing with some points in the article, and a reply from Bewley, in the course of which he says 'I think I had better present a detailed analysis of what the poem seems to mean.' This is what I wish he had done in the original article. I shall quote the analysis in full.

This poem seems to be a radical criticism of the conventionally wanton ethics of love that prevailed at the earlier Stuart Court, and which reached full flowering later in writers like Sir George Etherege and the Earl of Rochester. We only possess the stark outlines of Lovelace's career, but we know well enough that his experience of the milieu was immediate and protracted. The sentiments of most of his verse are representative of the fashion, but this poem is one of the occasions on which he seems to have had a sharp personal reaction. The first stanza begins by falling back on the seventeenth-century concern with death and progressive decay. The current belief that the world was in a cycle of deterioration, moving from a remote Golden Age towards an impending dissolution, was an implicit assumption behind such a poem as, say, Lovelace's 'Love Made in the First Age', where the theme is stated with conventional effectiveness, and in which decay and love are joined. The conjunction, I grant, is not unusual for the time; nevertheless I find the opening image of 'La Bella Bona-Roba' strange and personal, for the image of illicit erotic experience (the marmoset) is instantaneously and grotesquely transformed into a memento mori (the skeleton). Since a memento mori is an object for meditation, it still seems to me that the repeated 'bone' of the first stanza is meant to be a reflective repetition. There is a meditative withdrawal and shudder on the poet's part reflected in that repetition, and it is emphasized by his knowledge that he is almost alone in his reaction. The opening, 'I cannot tell who loves . . .' probably means 'I cannot measure or count the multitude . . .', or it may even mean, 'I cannot confess the following sentiments to my usual type of companion'. In such a reading the unusual grammatical compression, by no means a typical practice, causes the thought and phrasing to impinge with great directness on each other. If we were to read the sentence as a simple confession of unperspicacious ignorance it would be a very unconventional performance for a Carolinian courtier indeed. In the third line Lovelace begins to dissociate himself from the popular attitude. 'Give me a nakedness with her clothes on' has an immediacy in no way blunted by the fact that skin and clothes images were common in the seventeenth century. . . . The immediacy resides in the near-personification of 'a nakedness', a quality divorced from its subject and standing up in its own right, a self-existent entity. This immediacy is pressed home when one realizes the economy with which Lovelace is making an unusually complex statement in a minimum of words, and using conventional images for his own personal meaning. No contrast is intended between clothes and skin, for they are plainly identical. What Lovelace is asking for is a nakedness (physical love) that doesn't end with decay and death – that has no skeleton within – but which offers profounder fulfilment, which he symbolizes in the image of an interior nakedness replacing the skeleton, and hence triumphing over the memento mori of the opening figure. The second stanza relates to the enlarged physical appetites and capacities that characterized the men of the Golden Age, and which Lovelace describes in 'Love Made in the First Age'; and one might almost wonder if Lovelace were not simply regretting his own sensual limitations. But the appetites of the Golden Age were the reward of incorruption, and the third stanza of 'La Bella Bona-Roba' presents the desired fulfilment in terms of marriage, which it contrasts with the wasteful illicit love of stanzas 1 and 4. The man who establishes himself in marriage, consorting with a *single* love (aery lean) rather than with a flock of loves, repairs the damage inflicted on him in Eden, and is a complete person again. But the rake has none of these satisfactions, and is left with expenses and penalties as his reward. In the closing stanza the 'rascal deer', or lean deer that must be passed over, relate to the skeleton of the opening line, and the 'largest doe' relates to the fleshly ideal body of the second stanza.

So we are now in a position to know whether we agree with Bewley's reading of the poem or not. For my part, I don't find it persuasive; when I try to read the poem like that, it seems to fall apart. The suggestions of decay and death, though undeniably present in the poem, seem to me to be subordinate, not central. I don't find in the third stanza any indication of *marriage* offered as an ideal in contrast to wasteful illicit loves. 'Aery lean' does not seem to me to lend itself to the interpretation here imposed upon it – 'the man who establishes himself in marriage, consorting with a *single* love (aery lean) rather than with a flock of loves'. In short, I believe that Lovelace, or the speaker in the poem, is saying that he likes his women fat.

A marmoset was indeed a conventional term for a wanton woman; but it is also small-boned, and 'the skeleton of a poor marmoset' is a vivid visual representation of extreme thinness. The speaker finds it hard to believe that anybody could love a very thin woman – a nakedness altogether too naked: he prefers the bones to be decently clothed with flesh. 'Naught but bone, bone' registers the disappointed lover's progressive discovery – there is only one bone after another.

The preferred woman is more elaborately described in the second stanza: she is one who has some fleshly substance within the skin, and the analogy of flesh and clothing – in itself conventional – is developed with a precision and delight that are not at all conventional. The skin is a white satin upper coat – soft, smooth and white; it is lined with crimson velvet (and the etymology of 'incarnadin' goes back to the Latin for 'flesh'), which glows through the white satin and shows its colour plainly at the edges – lips, eyelids – as well as making the satin softer to be touch; and within these (insisted upon as a *sine qua non*) is a body of flesh, represented as a substantial inner garment, for 'body' has here the sense of 'bodice' as well as its modern meaning.

Yet some men do make love to thin women ('aery lean' must mean 'as thin as air'); and the explanation offered in the third stanza is deliberately far-fetched, as if to challenge the reader – 'Why else would they do it? Have you got a better suggestion?' It is that such men must be motivated by thrift: the cheapest way to recover their lost rib (the rib taken from Adam for the creation of Eve, and hence the inherited incompleteness of a man without a woman) seems to them to be to unite with a woman who is nothing but bone.

The huntsman in the fourth stanza is the man who hunts a woman; it is unfortunate for him ('Hard hap' is 'hard luck'), when he has assured himself of pneumatic bliss, if he finds no such thing when he comes to the point. The *assay* (a technical term in deer-hunting) was an incision made in the deer that had been killed, to ascertain how fat it was; and the keeper's fees were the portions of the prey customarily given to the gamekeeper. Both terms are used here with double meanings: 'After his 'say' is also 'after he has tried her out', and a 'keeper' was also a man who 'kept' a mistress.

The final stanza will now be clear enough. The speaker asks Cupid to discriminate, in respect of size – to ensure that only the largest woman shall be amorously attracted to him.

The ideal indicated, then, is primarily quantitative; 'the largest' in the last line is quite literal. But Stanza 2 transforms the poem – even, perhaps, makes it a poem. The intensity, there, of delight in the physical body involves a rich and delicate precision of response, well beyond the reach of what would ordinarily be called mere sensuality; flesh, and delight in it, can not be called 'mere' while we have that stanza in mind.

Bewley's reading of the poem is not only more edifying than mine – it is also more complex, and in certain ways more challenging. These may be reasons for preferring his reading; but I think there are stronger reasons against it. A version of the philosophical principle called Occam's razor can be applied (with proper caution) to the interpretation of poetry: the simpler explanation is to be preferred, provided it gives an adequate account of the facts. But here the reader must be the adjudicator – as, in the end, the reader always is.

Sometimes we can understand perfectly well what someone is saying, but not be at all sure what he means by it, or whether he means it. It is hardly surprising that in reading poetry – where we have only the printed words, unaided by tones of voice and facial expressions – we encounter this kind of difficulty more often than in conversation.

For many readers, the problem has been complicated by the way in which 'sincere' has been used too simply as a term of praise for poetry. John Donne, for example, is justly admired for liberating poetry from certain conventions and artificialities, and writing direct, forceful lines like

I wonder, by my troth, what thou and I
Did, till we loved?

and the word 'sincere' seems appropriate for describing their effect. Yet when we read on, we soon find ourselves struggling with some strenuous and ingenious argument, which with the best will in the world we can't quite believe in, or believe that the poet 'meant' quite seriously. In the tenth of the *Holy Sonnets*, which begins

Death be not proud, though some have called thee
Mighty and dreadful, for, thou art not so,

we find the fifth and sixth lines offering us this argument (still addressed to Death):

From rest and sleep, which but thy pictures be,
Much pleasure, then from thee, much more must flow.

We can't, I think, take this seriously as an argument, because, in the first place, we do not accept the premise that the relation between sleep and death is in all relevant respects the same as the relation between a picture and the thing depicted; and in the second place we can not for a moment believe that if a picture gives us pleasure the thing it depicts must necessarily give us more pleasure. Nor can we believe that Donne found this argument convincing, unless we suppose him to have been a person of mediocre intelligence – a supposition that would be hard to sustain while reading his poetry.

But this does not force us to conclude that Donne was being 'insincere' in writing this sonnet. It is perhaps the intrusion of the notion of 'sincerity' that tends to obscure our vision, and to prevent our seeing that the sonnet is a *dramatic* representation – an account, in the form of a dramatic monologue, of a man's struggles to overcome the fear of death. The imagined speaker clutches at straws of argument to sustain his bravado, and the weakness of their logic is part of the truth of the dramatic enactment of the man's (or of man's) predicament. He bravely hurls his puny weapons – some of them hardly more than insults – at his overpowering, all-devouring opponent, winning our appalled admiration but not the battle – until (and this is what makes the sonnet a 'holy' one) he falls back at last on Christ's victory over death:

One short sleep past, we wake eternally,
And death shall be no more, Death thou shalt die.

The contrast between the calm assurance of this and the desperate bravado of the other arguments is striking; but it could be missed if we insisted on looking for a simple kind of 'sincerity' in every part of the poem.

Most of Donne's *Songs and Sonets* are to some extent dramatic – that is, they represent what a person in an imagined situation might say or think. Donne, like Shakespeare, played many parts. There is a portrait of him in which he adopts the pose of the Melancholy Lover; and when he was near death he posed in his shroud for a sculptural representation of the resurrection of the dead. Of his poems, he once wrote in a letter to a friend,

You know my uttermost when it was best, and even then I
did best when I had least truth in my subject.

But there are kinds of truth that are best conveyed in fictions.
What truth, then, can we find in *The Flea*?

Mark but this flea, and mark in this,
How little that which thou deny'st me is;
Me it sucked first, and now sucks thee,
And in this flea, our two bloods mingled be;
Confess it, this cannot be said
A sin, or shame, or loss of maidenhead,
   Yet this enjoys before it woo,
    And pampered swells with one blood made of two,
    And this, alas, is more than we would do.

Oh stay, three lives in one flea spare,
Where we almost, nay more than married are.
This flea is you and I, and this
Our marriage bed, and marriage temple is;
Though parents grudge, and you, we're met,
And cloistered in these living walls of jet.
   Though use make you apt to kill me,
   Let not to this, self murder added be,
   And sacrilege, three sins in killing three.

Cruel and sudden, hast thou since
Purpled thy nail, in blood of innocence?
In what could this flea guilty be,
Except in that drop which it sucked from thee?
Yet thou triumph'st, and say'st that thou
Find'st not thyself, nor me the weaker now;

'Tis true, then learn how false, fears be;
Just so much honour, when thou yield'st to me,
Will waste, as this flea's death took life from thee.

It would be hard to find any single statement in this poem that
could aptly be described as 'sincere'. We have to take it, I think,
rather as if it were a scene from a play, without stage-directions.
The lovers are evidently together, both observing a flea in the
act of biting the lady – presumably on her wrist, if we suppose
her to be fully clothed. The opening lines of the poem parody
the rhetoric of the pulpit – the preacher introducing an
exemplum to clarify his exposition of a point of faith or
morals – and the argument that follows cannot be seriously
intended to convince the most moronic of ladies. That this one
is far from moronic soon becomes clear. The opening of the
second stanza indicates that she is about to express her
comment on the argument by killing the flea – a wholly apt
rejoinder, which shows that, far from being bewildered by the
argument, she is enjoying it. By now it is the mystery of
the Trinity that the parodied preacher is expounding; but the
rhetoric is modulating from that of the pulpit to that of the tragic
stage –

Oh stay, three lives in one flea spare

– and becomes wholly theatrical in the opening of the third
stanza. The argument that killing the flea would kill each of the
lovers is unanswerably refuted by the lady, who kills the flea
and observes that neither person is even weakened by the act.
The man then nicely displays his mastery of a mode of
argument often regarded as feminine: driven out of one
position, he magically reappears in the opposite one – "Tis true
. . .' – and attacks the lady's position from there. The movement of the argument has imitated that of a flea.

What is displayed here, then, is a playful and intimate conversation between a man and a woman, in which a lover's attempt
to persuade a lady is only one of the conventions they play with.
What the poem presents is argument as a form of love-play, and
a closer relation between 'heart' and 'mind' than Dryden
assumes when he complains that Donne

perplexes the minds of the fair sex with nice speculations of phi-
losophy, when he should engage their hearts, and entertain them with
the softnesses of love.

More to the point is Raquel Welch's observation that 'the mind is an erogenous zone'. The relationship briefly dramatized in this poem is more whole, and perhaps happier, than Dryden's vision of how a male poet should entertain the fair sex.

There is a poem by John Wilmot, Earl of Rochester, that a reader can hardly fail to understand as far as its paraphrasable content is concerned; but at least one critic has contrived to be very much mistaken as to what Rochester means by it. In *Lord Rochester's Monkey*, Graham Greene writes:

The spirit was always at war with the flesh: his unbelief was quite as religious as the Dean of St Pauls' faith. He hated the thing he loved with something of the same dark concentration, the confusion of love and lust and death and hate.

Let the porter and the groom,
  Things design'd for dirty slaves,
Drudge in fair Aurelia's womb,
  To get supplies for age and graves.

Even the single stanza that Mr Greene quotes would hardly support the assertions that precede it: there is a discrepancy of tone, at least, between them. Certainly the speaker in this stanza says that copulating with women is wearisome and unrewarding toil, and that if it needs to be done at all it ought to be left to the more muscular of the lower orders; but, on the evidence of this stanza alone, it is not at all clear that he means it. The fourth line says that the object of this activity is to provide more people to become old and fill graves – a motivation so improbable that we can not exclude the possibility that the speaker is joking, or playfully displaying his skill in arguing a paradox. If we now put the stanza in its context in the whole poem, that possibility gains strong confirmation:

Love a woman? You're an ass!
  'Tis a most insipid passion
To choose out for your happiness
  The silliest part of God's creation.

Let the porter and the groom,
  Things designed for dirty slaves,

Drudge in fair Aurelia's womb
  To get supplies for age and graves.

Farewell, woman! I intend
  Henceforth every night to sit
With my lewd, well-natured friend,
  Drinking to engender wit.

Then give me health, wealth, mirth, and wine,
  And, if busy love entrenches,
There's a sweet, soft page of mine
  Does the trick worth forty wenches.

The artful imitation of colloquial ease in the first stanza, where
the speaker cheerfully reproaches his friend for loving – of all
things – a woman, makes the nature of the joke clearer. By
stanza 3, where drinking is said to 'engender' wit in contrast to
sexual activity which can engender only people who become
old and die, the wholly unconvincing virtuosity of the argument
must surely make it unmistakable. The poem is clearly pro-
vocative, a song for teasing women; and the last stanza is the
final provocation, arguing that they are wholly unnecessary.

Teasing is a sociable activity, though there is often an
element of malice in it, and though it may (like tickling) touch
vulnerable spots. To fail to recognize a teasing tone, in poetry
as in conversation, is to be exposed to a good deal of
unnecessary embarrassment.

5 In Different Voices

And one man in his time plays may parts.
Shakespeare, *As You Like it*, Act 2 Scene 7

Milton's *Lycidas*, in which 'the Author bewails a learned Friend, unfortunatly drown'd in his Passage from *Chester* on the *Irish* Seas, 1637,' begins with these lines:

Yet once more, O ye Laurels, and once more
Ye Myrtles brown, with Ivy never-sear,
I com to pluck your Berries harsh and crude,
And with forc'd fingers rude,
Shatter your leaves before the mellowing year.
Bitter constraint, and sad occasion dear,
Compels me to disturb your season due:
For *Lycidas* is dead, dead ere his prime
Young *Lycidas*, and hath not left his peer . . .

In reading this we are unlikely to entertain for a moment the supposition that these words record an apology addressed by John Milton to some laurels and myrtles, on the occasion of his taking berries and leaves from them to make a wreath for his dead friend. Rather, the poet has deliberately adopted a certain voice as appropriate to his present purpose; a voice that seems intended to disguise his individuality like a ritual mask. It is the 'speech' of an actor, a public declamation rather than a personal and private meditation; and the laurels and myrtles are there to define the role: the learned poet in the classical pastoral tradition, where the people spoken of are represented as shepherds and their setting as rural. (In the closing lines of *Lycidas*, all that has gone before is attributed to an 'uncouth Swain', 'warbling his Dorick lay'.) In choosing to write in this way, Milton is not merely displaying his own erudition; he is drawing on the studies that Edward King has shared with him, and adopting a voice appropriate for a public lament for a scholar.

I do not propose to enter into a fuller discussion of *Lycidas*; I have used these lines only to suggest what I mean by the 'voice' a poet adopts. In this case it is a highly artificial construction, devised not only to enable the poem to say some things that could not be said so effectively in a more 'natural' voice – conversational or meditative, for example – but also because the voice itself conveys something about Edward King and how his death is to be regarded.

If Milton elsewhere adopts a less elevated voice, it may be no less calculated, no less deliberately chosen for its appropriateness to the subject. His poem on the death of Hobson, the university carrier, who hired out horses and drove a coach between Cambridge and London, is public on a smaller scale than *Lycidas*; it commemorates a well known Cambridge character, but not one whose death could appropriately be treated as a national misfortune, a grave loss to scholarship and the church. (As it turns out, Edward King is now quite forgotten except as the subject of *Lycidas*, whereas Hobson's name remains familiar in the phrase 'Hobson's choice': those who went to his stables to hire a horse were free to choose – they could take the one next to the door or go without.)

On the University Carrier
who sick'nd in the time of his vacancy, being
forbid to go to *London*, by reason of the Plague

Here lies old *Hobson*, Death hath broke his girt,
And here alas, hath laid him in the dirt,
Or els the ways being foul, twenty to-one,
He's here stuck in a slough, and overthrown.
'Twas such a shifter, that if truth were known,
Death was half glad when he had got him down;
For he had any time this ten years full,
Dodg'd with him, betwixt *Cambridge* and the Bull.
And surely, Death could never have prevail'd,
Had not his weekly cours of carriage fail'd;
But lately finding him so long at home,
And thinking now his journeys end was come,

And that he had tane up his latest Inne,
In the kind office of a Chamberlin
Shew'd him his room where he must lodge that night,
Pull'd off his Boots, and took away the light:
If any ask for him, it shall be sed,
Hobson has supt, and 's newly gon to bed.

In *Lycidas* the man whose death is mourned had enough in
common with Milton to make him think of his own death – an
association of ideas that has perhaps some part in every meditation on another's death. As Donne puts it,

No man is an *Iland*, intire of it selfe; every man is a peece of the
Continent, a part of the *maine*; if a *Clod* bee washed away by the *Sea*,
Europe is the lesse, as well as if a *Promontorie* were, as well as if a
Mannor of thy *friends*, or of *thine owne* were; Any Mans *death*
diminishes *me*, because I am involved in *Mankinde*; And therefore
never send to know for whom the *bell* tolls; It tolls for *thee*.

But it is possible for the transfer of concern from the other
person's death to one's own expected death to become an
evasion of the reality of the other's death, a merely selfish
anxiety. In the poem on Hobson, Milton leaves himself out of it
entirely, and directs our attention to the uniqueness of the man
who is commemorated: he honours the otherness of Hobson.
However unimaginable another's experience of death must be,
and however unknowable one's own, one thing at least we can
be sure of: Hobson's death would be nothing like Milton's.
Hobson's death, the language of the poem firmly reminds us, is
his very own; and it would be wrong for any poet or preacher to
try to appropriate it by telling it in classical or religious terms
that were no part of Hobson. Horses and coaches, muddy roads
and inns, an occasional bet at twenty to one, are such terms as
Hobson dealt with his world in; they were the material of his
life, so how else should his death be spoken of?

There is no solemnity in the poem – and this too seems to
indicate the poet's respect for the man himself: it would be a
foolish condescension to be more solemn about him than he
was himself. Yet, without any grave thoughts or elevated
diction to work up solemnity, the closing lines of the poem do
make his death as serious and moving a matter, in his own
terms, as the death of a well known and irreplaceable person
should be.

This is a much simpler poem than *Lycidas* in many respects. For the voice of *Lycidas* modulates through several moods, from quiet regret to anger and indignation; the shepherd is also a Christian 'pastor'; the pastoral scene is far from idyllic; and even the elegiac smoothness of the opening lines has to accommodate the energy of the imagined onslaught in 'shatter your leaves' – a startling ferocity of diction that recurs throughout the poem. In comparison, the poem *On the University Carrier* is all of a piece, and invites no strenuous intellectual activity. Yet when we try to read it aloud, we find that trying to find the right voice for it is more challenging, more interesting and strangely more rewarding than trying to read 'Lycidas' aloud. It seems that we must try to imagine, to recreate from the poem, how Hobson spoke – yet not in order to imitate his speech: rather to interpret the indications the poem gives us of how people who knew Hobson would naturally speak about him. There is a sustained play of metaphor and double meaning throughout the poem that is distinctly not Hobson's; yet Hobson's own speech seems always to be in mind as a controlling principle. There is something of the wit of a group of students in the sustaining of the word-play – yet it isn't a joke, and its treatment of Hobson is not at all patronizing. The many achievements of *Lycidas* seem calculated – whatever we discover in that poem, we can be pretty sure that the poet deliberately worked it out and put it there; and as readers we either understand what he is doing or we don't, and in so far as we do, the reading aloud demands only competence. The voice of *On the University Carrier*, on the other hand, is responsive to Hobson, rather than calculated to be appropriate to him; it conveys a sense of the man rather than knowledge about him; and reading it aloud is a correspondingly subtle undertaking, calling upon intuitive responses to linguistic signals that we can not be fully conscious of. In this, it is a more dramatic poem, its use of language more like Shakespeare's, than *Lycidas*.

The next poem, too, provides an interesting example of the use of a particular voice as part of the whole meaning of a poem. Perhaps it is not just a coincidence that it should be another epitaph; for even in conversation, talking about someone who has recently died can often be difficult, and we are conscious of the difficulty as a matter of striking the right note, getting the tone of voice right, when there are so many ways in which it can be false. Clichés about death come so easily to mind; and though they have all probably been useful (or they would not have become clichés), there is a sense in which they hinder our response to this particular death, which is unique and absolute.

As Milton records the uniqueness of Hobson's death, so Ben Jonson, in a very different poem, focuses the uniqueness of the death of Salamon Pavey, a boy actor.

Epitaph on S.P., a Child of Queen Elizabeth's Chapel

Weep with me all you that read
   This little story:
And know, for whom a tear you shed,
   Death's self is sorry.
'Twas a child, that so did thrive
   In grace, and feature,
As Heaven and Nature seemed to strive
   Which owned the creature.
Years he numbered scarce thirteen
   When Fates turned cruel,
Yet three filled zodiacs had he been
   The stage's jewel;
And did act (what now we moan)
   Old men so duly,
As, sooth, the Parcae thought him one,
   He played so truly.
So, by error, to his fate
   They all consented;
But viewing him since (alas, too late)
   They have repented.
And have sought (to give new birth)
   In baths to steep him;
But, being so much too good for earth,
   Heaven vows to keep him.

What the fanciful narrative conveys is a tribute to an accomplished professional actor; and by giving the tribute the form of a 'little story', Jonson keeps in mind the fact that his late colleague was also a child. His death is described as a victory for Heaven over Nature: Salamon's merits have been such that it has been doubtful whether he belonged to the realm of ideal perfection – Heaven – or to the world of flawed reality – Nature; and in the end he has been kept by Heaven because he was 'so much too good for earth'. 'Good' seems to refer to his professional qualities rather than his moral virtues, though they may have their part in the rich ambiguity of the word 'grace'; the boy was too good an actor to be allowed to return to earth, to the realm of Nature, in spite of the tears that were shed for him as if they were contributions to a reviving bath, a cauldron of rebirth. (If there is a more specific allusion here it is probably to Æson, Jason's father, rejuvenated by Medea by boiling in a magic herbal bath.) If the 'little story' that the opening of the poem invited us to hear has proved to be rather different from what we might have expected, alluding to things that children are not usually familiar with and following a more fanciful course than we might feel appropriate to the gravity of the occasion, that should again remind us that the boy actor, who probably had some Seneca in his repertoire, would be familiar with classical allusions, and with fictions – however improbable – taken seriously as vehicles for emotional and imaginative experience.

The awareness of S.P.'s uniqueness is what makes the poem remain, even today, as a monument; millions have died and millions have mourned, but there has not been and could not be another Salamon Pavey as this poem celebrates him. The tribute to a respected colleague and the tender regret for a child who died are the two co-ordinates that locate this uniqueness. This combination is present in the whole texture of the poem; it is even, I think, in the metre, the alternation of long and short lines, where generally the long lines have something of the resonance of the public language of the stage, and the short ones suggest the simpler, more homely tones in which one might speak to, or about, a child. Not that every pair of long and short lines is sharply differentiated – that would have been to deny the fact (and the wonder) that the child and the actor were one person. But in the first line, although the words are simple, the gesture and the voice are theatrical, quite appropriately so, and 'all you' addresses a gathered audience such as S.P. had often declaimed to; while 'This little story' is altogether more suggestive of the child as child, off the stage. The following pairs of lines don't need to overdo this contrast; the double vision established in the opening is kept in play by maintaining the metre, and just suggesting a more relaxed, more conversational tone in the short lines.

As in Milton's poem, then, this poem's evocation of a voice (or voices) has an important part in identifying and keeping alive the memory of a special, distinctive life ended by a death that could be nobody else's.

George Herbert, in *The Quip*, uses changes of voice in a more obviously dramatic way, and here again the full meaning of the poem can hardly be grasped without trying to read it aloud and thus becoming aware of the problems involved in striking the right note.

The Quip

The merrie World did on a day
With his train-bands and mates agree
To meet together where I lay,
And all in sport to geere at me.

First Beautie crept into a rose,
Which when I pluckt not, 'Sir,' said she,
'Tell me, I pray, whose hands are those?'
But Thou shalt answer, Lord, for me.

Then Money came, and chinking still,
'What tune is this, poore man?' said he;
'I heard in Musick you had skill';
But Thou shalt answer, Lord, for me.

Then came brave Glorie puffing by
In silks that whistled, who but he!
He scarce allowed me half an eie:
But Thou shalt answer, Lord, for me.

Then came quick Wit and Conversation,
And he would needs a comfort be,
And, to be short, make an oration:
But Thou shalt answer, Lord, for me.

Yet when the houre of Thy designe
To answer these fine things shall come,
Speak not at large, say, I am Thine,
And then they have their answer home.

'The World' in this context personifies the whole body of worldly values as opposed to the renunciations and austerities of the religious life, one of the traditional trio of impediments to salvation: the World, the Flesh and the Devil. His train-bands would be his trained militia – part-time soldiers perhaps, but with some skill in the ways of the world. Right from the start, however, we are made aware that the traditional image of the World (from the religious person's point of view) is significantly modified in this poem: it is not seen as overtly menacing and destructive, but as 'The merrie World'; and although it conspires maliciously, the malice seems incidental to the fun: 'all in sport to geere at me.' The speaker, who is the victim of the jest, is not complaining bitterly against it – rather, he seems disposed to excuse it as far as he can.

Just how attractively the successive mockers are presented becomes clear if we recognize this poem as being in the tradition of the medieval pageants of the Seven Deadly Sins, and of the many sermons, poems and aids to reflection designed to help the Christian to arrive at a contempt for the things of the world: Beautie, Money and Glorie in this poem represent the sins of Lust, Avarice and Pride. But to give them those bad names would be to suggest that one sees them as repulsive (and that one is consequently in little danger of being seduced by them). There is an engaging ambivalence in this poem's treatment of them – reflecting an awareness of the world as delightful as well as dangerous.

It is certainly delight that is uppermost in 'Beautie crept into a rose', and the poem invites us to admire the delicacy of the mocking temptation. For Beautie speaks with the voice of an archly teasing woman; her seemingly innocent question carries the implication that she knows perfectly well what he would like to do with his hands, but that he is making as little use of them as if they were not his; teasing, too, in offering the opportunity for the easily gallant answer – 'Yours, madam, at your service.' That the speaker of the poem would not be at a loss for an appropriately witty and courteous refusal is clear enough too, and in forgoing the satisfaction of giving it he is affirming his total dependence – his choosing to be totally dependent – on God: for to reply, however virtuously and tactfully, in such a way would be to take pride in his own 'quick Wit and Conversation'. He turns away – as if with a rueful smile, acknowledging the wit of the mockery of himself – not only from the woman, but from the 'worldly' mode of discourse.

The rich man who personifies the lure of Money is one who enjoys, rather than obsessively hoards, his wealth; and his ingeniously devious mockery of the narrator is presented to us in the manner of one who, reporting a joke against himself, acknowledges a palpable hit. But again he abstains from answering, choosing instead to rest on the assurance that his master will answer for him.

'Glorie' is again a more attractive version of 'Pride' ('brave' means 'fine' here); and both his splendour and his own consciousness of it are suggested in the second line – 'In silks that whistled, who but he!' *His* mockery of the narrator is expressed not in words but in hardly deigning to look at him – but this, too, requires an answer. What has become clear by now, I think, is that any answer the narrator could make to his mockers would have to be in their language, the language of worldly values, if it were to be effective in silencing their mockery: he would have to play their games. This, perhaps, is the temptation that is hardest for him to resist.

Although 'quick Wit and Conversation' do not in themselves correspond to any of the traditional 'seven deadly sins', as we have seen they are here closely associated with pride, and their place in the group is fully justified. They are the form in which the secondary temptation comes, once the others are resisted – the temptation to triumph over the other temptations by answering them wittily in their own terms. This fourth member of the 'merry World''s militia is treated with far less appreciation, and more explicit rejection, than the others: 'he *would needs* a comfort be' suggests a foolishly inappropriate insistence, and the orator's cliché 'to be short' is ridiculed. If we suspect from this that the tempter of this stanza is felt by the narrator to be more of a threat to him than the others were, so that he cannot afford to be as generously appreciative as he has been of the others, we may gain some support for our suspicion from the fact that the poet had held the post of University Orator before becoming a parish priest.

The final stanza indicates the answer that all the mockeries require: that the narrator serves another master, who is lord of all that the mockers think they have – the beauty of the Rose of Sharon; the Kingdom, the Power, and the Glory. . . . But such an answer from the narrator would only expose him to further mockery, wittily hinting that this unseen master evidently keeps his servants on a pretty slender allowance of all these delights. To be effective, the answer must come from the master himself, in his own good time; 'the houre' is perhaps the hour of the last judgement. Only thus could there be an answer that would silence the mockers.

I have suggested that 'the World' belongs to the trio of 'the World, the Flesh, and the Devil'. But the Christian narrator in this poem does not treat it with the grim hostility that some versions of piety would require. He is reporting to God (to whom the whole poem is addressed); and he asks for no vengeance on his persecutors. His tone is nearer to that of 'Father, forgive them, for they know not what they do.' And it is not fanciful to suppose that he also has in mind that 'God so loved the world, that he gave his only begotten son. . . .'

The voice of the poem, then, is a complex one, and the simplicity of the words should not lead us to underestimate the subtlety of its meaning – of which that voice, and of other voices contained in it, are an essential part.

When we listen to somebody speaking, a good deal of our understanding of the speaker's meaning comes from our response to the sound of the voice. We may be aware of a quiet earnestness, a vehemence, a shrillness of over-emphasis, or a momentary tremor in an otherwise steady voice. But there are more subtle qualities that we respond to without being quite conscious of them, clues that are given and received without the knowledge and control of hearer or speaker. For the voice necessarily registers something of the body that produces it, a body that is inseparable from the emotions that inhabit it. So the production of the voice is affected by the relative tensions and relaxations of muscles in the diaphragm, chest, throat and mouth, by the rate and regularity and force of breathing and heartbeat. The listener, having a body similarly constructed and subject to the same disturbances, interprets the clues in the voice intuitively: it is one of the ways in which we know more than we know we know.

The reader, on the other hand, is deprived of such clues. This is the most obvious disadvantage of written, as against spoken, communication. (Of course it can be an advantage if one is trying to conceal one's feelings, but it is then more than ever a disadvantage for the listener.)

So it may well seem strange that I have been referring to the 'voice' of a poem, and even to a poem's having several 'voices' – even more strange if the reader has not found this attribution meaningless. What it does mean is that a poem, using the varied resources of language available to it, can give the reader a remarkably subtle sense of a living voice, a voice that one tries, in reading aloud, to recapture, to reconstitute in one's own body. In so far as this can be achieved, one reconstitutes also some sense of the factors that condition such a voice – the emotional state and the outward circumstances that would cause a voice to be like that.

My next illustration is another poem by George Herbert.

The Collar

I struck the board, and cry'd, 'No more;
    I will abroad.'
  What, shall I ever sigh and pine?
My lines and life are free; free as the road,
  Loose as the winde, as large as store.
     Shall I be still in suit?
  Have I no harvest but a thorn
  To let me bloud, and not restore
What I have lost with cordiall fruit?
     Sure there was wine
  Before my sighs did drie it; there was corn
   Before my tears did drown it;
  Is the yeare onely lost to me?
   Have I no bayes to crown it,
No flowers, no garlands gay? all blasted,
    All wasted?
  Not so, my heart; but there is fruit,
    And thou hast hands.
  Recover all thy sigh-blown age
On double pleasures; leave thy cold dispute
Of what is fit and not; forsake thy cage,
    Thy rope of sands
Which pettie thoughts have made; and made to thee
  Good cable, to enforce and draw,
    And be thy law,
  While thou didst wink and wouldst not see.
    Away! take heed;
    I will abroad.

Call in thy death's-head there, tie up thy fears;
    He that forbears
  To suit and serve his need
    Deserves his load.
But as I rav'd and grew more fierce and wilde
    At every word,
  Methought I heard one calling, 'Childe';
    And I reply'd, 'My Lord.'

Here the poet does full justice to the argument that no great man's dependant would tolerate from his patron the treatment that a Christian endures from his god; and he offers no counter-argument. Instead, he redefines the context of the argument so that it is seen to be beside the point – not invalid but irrelevant.

The speaker argues – or rather, protests vehemently – that there is a limit to the reasonableness of enduring and renouncing, and that he has reached that limit. There is nothing to prevent him from going wherever he pleases – 'My lines and life are free. . . .' He has nothing to show for all his renunciation, no earnest of reward or recognition; and he recalls that his prospects had not been barren before he gave them up to follow this ungenerous master: 'Sure there was wine/ Before my sighs did drie it. . . .' This leads him to the reflection that his former prospects are still not beyond his reach: life still has joys to offer, once he can bring himself to cast off his present servitude. He can still make up for the time he has lost – 'Recover all thy sigh-blown age/ On double pleasures. . . .' The restraints that hold him are illusory – existing only in his own mind: 'Thy rope of sands,/ Which pettie thoughts have made. . . .' He defies the sanctions, as if he were calling on the master of the house to chain up his toothless dogs – 'Call in thy death's-head there, tie up thy fears. . . .' And finally he reminds himself, as a last spur to his resolution, that if he *doesn't* walk out when nothing is to be gained by staying, and all the delights of life to be gained by leaving, he will deserve all that he endures.

The argument is whole and convincing, and in its own terms unanswerable. But such an argument must have a context, and this one has a vividly dramatized situation in which it exists, both in the clue of the opening line and in the tone of the whole, the voice that it implies. The vehemence of the reported action, 'I struck the board', is sustained in the forceful plain speaking that follows, the exaggerated images of sighs that dried the wine, tears that drowned the corn, the time spent in service blasted, wasted, 'sigh-blown' (coined from 'fly-blown', infested with maggots). Such words can hardly be spoken unemphatically. The lines maintain an iambic pattern that is used to the full to control and accentuate the emphasis, while varying in length from two to five stresses in a way that suggests, even mimics, the varying rhythms of forceful rhetorical speech. And if 'rhetorical' suggests a working-up of feeling that is not purely or simply spontaneous, that suggestion is reinforced by the way rhyme answers rhyme with careful irregularity.

What these features together seem to indicate is the rehearsed spontaneity of one who says, 'I went to the boss and I told him straight. . . .' By the time we are half way through the monologue we may imagine the listeners saying, 'Yes, yes, and what did he say to *that*?' But then, with 'Not so, my heart,' it becomes clear for the first time that the speaker was not shouting all this to the face of the boss, but sitting by himself in the kitchen thinking out what he *would* tell him straight; he is talking to himself, and in that context striking the board seems a very different gesture.

The context changes again, dramatically and decisively, in the last four lines. The change is not obvious in the appearance of the lines on the page: they seem at first sight to continue the irregularity of the rest of the poem. But in fact they form a far more regular unit, a four-lined stanza (though the lines that rhyme together are of different lengths); with a clear and very simple pattern of rhymes and a more even, undisturbed rhythm. The vehemence is gone; the voice in which that vehemence is accurately reported ('as I rav'd and grew more fierce and wild/ At every word') is a calm one. What it narrates is, on one level, an experience that most people have had: when the moment for confrontation arrives, one never can remember all the things one was going to say. But, more unexpectedly, it turns out at last that the boss is not only the speaker's lord but also his father; in the end the passionate protestor is seen as if he were about seven years old, threatening to leave home. The arguments have not been answered; but they have been relocated in the context of a relationship that transcends them, and the speaker has acknowledged this. It is not only the twist at the end of the story that makes the point, but the change of voice in the final quatrain, where a steady, assured 'reasonableness' contrasts with, and places, the excited 'reasonings' of the earlier part.

Blake's *Songs of Innocence* and *Songs of Experience* are col-
lections of poems that seem to require a large number of different voices. A few of them may be thought of as spoken
directly by the poet, who perhaps claims for his own voice
something of the visionary authority of the bard in Celtic tradition – inspired, prophetic, a messenger of gods and spirits.
His introduction to the *Songs of Experience* begins:

Hear the voice of the Bard!
Who Present, Past, & Future, sees;
Whose ears have heard
The Holy Word
That walk'd among the ancient trees.

But most of the *Songs* seem to be spoken by imagined cha-
racters – a baby, a schoolboy, a nurse, and several who are not
so clearly identified. An interesting example is *A Poison Tree* in
Songs of Experience:

I was angry with my friend,
I told my wrath, my wrath did end;
I was angry with my foe,
I told it not, my wrath did grow.

And I water'd it in fears,
Night & morning with my tears;
And I sunned it with smiles,
And with soft deceitful wiles.

And it grew both day and night,
Till it bore an apple bright;
And my foe beheld it shine,
And he knew that it was mine,

And into my garden stole
When the night had veil'd the pole:
In the morning glad I see
My foe outstretch'd beneath the tree.

In spite of the first-person narrative, the first stanza doesn't
really sound like somebody telling us about a personal experience. The strictly parallel constructions of the two halves of
the stanza suggest that a process of analysis and generalization

lies behind it; what we have is a concise statement of a pattern observed in, probably, many individual experiences – the 'I' is used impersonally, and the voice has a scientist's detachment as it gives us, concisely and precisely, a statement of the consequences of repressing hostile feelings.

But then something changes. In the second and later stanzas the 'I' is still there, but no longer impersonally – now it is intensely personal, and the voice is that of a maniac's confession, confident that his appalled hearers will approve and admire his cunning strategy and its triumphant outcome. At the same time the large proportion of lines starting with 'And' suggests the headlong progress of the story and the eagerness of the telling, as well as making the succession of events seem to have no necessary or discernible connection of cause and effect – they follow each other like events in a dream, and the growth of the poison tree is made to seem mysterious, magical. The narrative is not an *allegory*, because that would require that the growth of the Poison Tree could be 'translated', step by step, into a literal account of how repressed anger leads to destruction; but it is *symbolic* of that process. A symbol need not have a known relationship to something else that it stands for; but it does here suggest the nature of the process by which the wrath is cherished, and eventually bears fruit which proves deadly. That process is also characterized by the nature of the voice which we imagine telling the story.

Reading the poem attentively, and recognizing that the way events follow each other in it is something we have experienced in our dreams, we may come to see that that voice is not wholly unfamiliar to us either: in some circumstances, in some kind of dream, it could be our own voice. If a poem can bring about such self-knowledge, the study of poetry must be taken seriously.

Index

Allegory, 72
Ambiguity, 20, 24, 44, 51, 52, 63
As You Like It, 58

Ballade, 4
Bardic tradition, 21, 71
Belinda, 5
Bewley, Marius, 47–50
Binocular vision, 14
Blake, William, 3, 13–15, 71–2
Blank verse, 2

Canterbury Tales, 2
Chaucer, 2, 3
Cinematic effects, 35
Clod and the Pebble, The, 13–15
Collar, The, 68–70
Contradictory truths, 13–16
Conventions, 7–9, 51–2, 55

Dactyls, 1
Dickinson, Emily, 6
Dish of Peaches in Russia, A, 43–7
Donne, John, 12, 22, 31, 42, 52–6, 60
Dramatic monologue, 53, 70
Dryden, John, 55–6

Easter 1916, 3, 17–21
Edgeworth, Maria, 5
Eliot, T. S., 2
Epitaph on S. P., 62–4

Faerie Queene, The, 2
Flea, The, 54–6
Free verse, 2, 36–7
Frost, Robert, 5

Greene, Graham, 56

Habit of Perfection, The, 38–41
Hamlet, 23, 25–6
. *Henry IV Part 1*, 15–16
Herbert, George, 31, 64–70
Heroic couplet, 3
Holy Sonnet X, 53–4
Hopkins, Gerard Manley, 38–41

Iambic pentameter, 2
Iambic tetrameter, 28
Imaginative experience, 12–13
Implicit imagery, 25
Intonation, 26
I sing of a maiden, 3, 33

Jonson, Ben, 62–4

Kangaroo, 2, 36–7

La Bella Bona-Roba, 47–52
Landowska, Wanda, 32
Lawrence, D. H., 1, 2, 36–7
Longfellow, Henry Wadsworth, 4
Lovelace, Richard, 47–52
Line ending, 29, 30
Lord Rochester's Monkey, 56
Lycidas, 58–61
Lyric, 33

Macbeth, 26
Marvell, Andrew, 23, 27–32, 42
Metaphysical poetry, 31
Metre, 2
Milton, John, 2, 3, 58–61

Naming of Parts, 1

Occam's razor, 52

Octave, 3
Octet, 3
Othello, 22

Paradise Lost, 2
Parody, 55
Petrarchan sonnet, 3
Poison Tree, A, 3, 71–2
Pope, Alexander, 2, 3
Pound, Ezra, 4
Prelude, The, 2
Prepositions, stressed, 32
Prose, 1
Psalm 23, 39
Pun, 11–12

Quip, The, 64–7

Radio commentators, 32
Rainbow, The, 1
Reading aloud, 26–9, 32–3, 37, 40, 61, 63, 64, 68
Realized imagery, 23, 41
Reed, Henry, 1
Repetition, 34
Revenger's Tragedy, The, 2, 23–5
Rondeau, 4
Royal Shakespeare Company, 26

Satire III, 22
Scepticism, 19
Scrutiny, 47
Sermon preached at St Paul's, Christmas Day 1621, 42
Sestet, 3

Sestina, 4
Shakespeare, William, 2, 8–12, 15–16, 22, 23, 26, 33, 58
Shakespearean sonnet, 3
Sincerity, 52–5
Song of Hiawatha, The, 4
Songs and Sonets, 54
Songs of Experience, 71
Songs of Innocence, 71
Sonnet, 3
Sonnet 130, 8
Sonnet 138, 10
Spenser, Edmund, 2
Spondees, 1
Stanza, 3
Stevens, Wallace, 43–7
Symbol, 72

Teasing, 57, 65
Theology and poetry, 35–6
To His Coy Mistress, 27–32, 42
Tourneur, Cyril, 2, 23–5
Triple Fool, The, 12
Trochaic tetrameter, 4

University Carrier, On the, 3, 59–61

Verse, 1

Waste Land, The, 2
Welch, Raquel, 56
Wilmot, John, Earl of Rochester, 56–7
Wordsworth, William, 2

Yeats, W. B., 3, 17–21